Small Scale Gardening

Small Scale Gardening

Leslie Johns

WILLOW BOOKS
Collins
8 Grafton Street, London
1984

To Jenny,
with love

Willow Books
William Collins Sons & Co Ltd
London · Glasgow · Sydney
Auckland · Toronto · Johannesburg

First published in Great Britain 1984

Cover illustration by Gillian Platt
Illustrations throughout by Patti Pearce of The Garden Studio
Book design by John Gordon
Cover design by Cloud Nine Design
Small Scale Gardening was conceived and edited by Smart Associates
16 Spencer Gardens, London SW14 7AH

Johns, Leslie
Small scale gardening
1. Gardening 2. Gardens–Design
I. Title
712'.6 SB453

ISBN 0 00 218094 4

Typesetting by V & M Graphics Ltd, Aylesbury, Bucks
Colour reproduction by Lithospeed Ltd, London
Printed in Spain by Printer Industria Grafica SA, Barcelona

D.L.B. 97-1984

CONTENTS

INTRODUCTION

♦

It is encouraging to realize that given the opportunity — some soil, some moisture and some light — a plant will grow. It is a simple matter for anyone, whether a skilled or inexperienced gardener, to have a decorative plant growing through balcony railings, flowers in full bloom bursting in a vibrant splash of colour from an upper window box, or even a crop of tomatoes blushing into appetizing colour on a tiny city patio.

Gardening on a small scale really is easy. Remember that it's a natural thing for seeds to germinate, for seedlings to develop, for plants to reach upwards, put out their leaves and their flowers. They do it in the wild and they will do it for you. Not every plant will always grow to be a perfect specimen, but the important thing is to have something growing, some evidence of the natural order when everything around you is a stone and concrete denial of the burgeoning green that is the basis of life — and has been for many thousands of years.

It's a marvellous thing, the fact that plants will grow divorced completely from all the benefits, indeed from the necessities, of mother earth. They will grow in a small pot, trough, bowl, basket, bag, box or other container. They will grow in an artificial soil. They will grow in a space which seems incredibly small. And because they will accept such confined root space they will, in turn, limit the height and spread of their growth above the soil. After three years in a tub a shrub may still be less than a metre (3ft) tall, whereas planted in a garden it might have grown to twice that height.

There are many advantages in growing plants in small spaces, many more than the simple pleasure of watching leaves and flowers change and develop according to season. It is perfectly possible to grow food, for example. Lettuces and radishes will grow well, quickly, easily in a window box. Tomatoes will ripen in a growbag. Some herbs will mature in plastic pots, strawberries in a barrel, as indeed will potatoes, but do not expect to feed the family for the summer. Instead, look forward to the undoubted extra flavour from your small harvest of fresh produce.

Another delight in store for the small scale gardener with a patio, balcony or rooftop of plants — and sometimes with only a flower-filled window box — is the added unexpected gift of butterflies and bees, even in the centre of a city.

I do not produce these statements of fact out of the air. I do not make claims that I cannot substantiate. Today, I cultivate an over-large garden in the rural and unspoilt countryside, but for something like 20 years I grew my plants in the centre of London. In the hub of what was then Covent Garden's fruit and vegetable market, flowers flourished in a long balcony trough on one floor, while the roof at the top of the building was almost hidden with herbaceous plants of almost every kind and colour, with shrubs of strength and beauty, with two or three shade-providing trees and even a few rampant climbers, such as a passion fruit and a Russian vine. It was a wonderful experience of gardening on a small scale and it establishes, I trust, my credentials in presuming to put this little book into your hands.

Leslie Johns

Small Scale Gardening
PART I

BALCONY AND PATIO GARDENS

♦

Initially, there would seem to be little comparison for the purposes of growing plants for pleasure between a patio at ground level and a balcony up in the air. Yet there are so many similarities that we can consider them together, looking at the differences once we have examined the advantages they may have in common.

To say that we have space for elaborate gardening on a patio or a balcony would be, perhaps, to exaggerate, but it would be true to say that we have more space in both places than we would have were we gardening merely in a window box, a pot or two, or perhaps even a hanging basket. Probably the most important advantage is that we have floor space. It is possible to put down a trough on the floor, even a series of troughs, and in most cases it is also possible to erect another trough, or some similar container, on the wall or fence above the first. In other words, we have the possibility of gardening in two dimensions.

So long as there is space to tend the growing plants and space to enjoy them, the remainder of the area can be occupied by the vegetation itself, always bearing in mind that this growing green should not be so dense that it darkens the inside of the house.

One essential difference between balcony and patio should be pointed out right away, for it is of vital importance. No balcony gardening should be enjoyed or even considered until you are absolutely certain that the balcony itself is strong enough to bear the considerable weight that can be placed on it by the number of pots and troughs with their plants. It is possible to obtain lightweight containers, which should always be used on a balcony in preference to heavy materials such as stone or terracotta, but it is the weight of the soil or planting medium, particularly when wet, that is the determining factor.

The weight of water alone is normally calculated at roughly 4.5kg (10lbs) per 4.5 litres (1gal). A single trough of plants can easily absorb 9 litres (2gal) which, with the weight of the soil and that of the plants, can mean that the total for this single trough can bear down on the balcony with a pressure of something like 25kg (half a hundredweight). If the space is well filled with tubs, pots or other containers, all filled with lushly growing plants, all well moistened as is vital to good growth, then the weight can be such as seriously to strain the balcony's supports. Make sure, therefore, that any balcony is strong enough to support very considerable weight before you load it with materials for which it was not, after all, originally built.

Most balconies have an integral drainage system. In time of heavy rain the water does not merely collect or drip to the ground over its edge, but runs away through purpose-built drains. This is as it should be. But bear in mind that balconies, because they are up in the air, are normally subjected to stronger winds than prevail at ground level. This can mean that when watering your plants with a hose you can quite inadvertently spray the windows of a neighbouring building or deposit drips on to the heads of the astonished passers-by in the street below. A balcony glowing with living colour can be a delight to all who behold it, but the glamour somehow goes if one has to dodge the drips.

The strong winds that occasionally buffet a balcony can also mean that leaves, garden rubbish or even soil can sometimes be blown onto or even into neighbouring buildings. And this raises one point of the utmost importance in all gardening on a small scale. Where space is so limited there is no room for rubbish. All spilled soil, all fallen leaves, all dead-headed flowers, all prunings, should be carefully and meticulously placed inside some container where they cannot fly free in a puff of wind. It is helpful to carry around with you a plastic sack or lightweight bucket while you carry out your daily tending and watering, and place any garden detritus in it. This serves

A balcony glowing with living colour, but because plants are more exposed to strong winds than on a patio, any climbers – such as the rose and vine above – must be secured to a trellis and window boxes held firmly in place.

two purposes: in the first place you avoid causing annoyance to local citizens and, equally important, you eliminate the dangers caused by little heaps of leaves or soil which are so often the breeding ground of insects and plant diseases.

So the motto for all small scale gardeners should be *keep it clean*. Remember that a balcony or patio is a garden in miniature and that each plant in or on it has the relative importance of a large tree in a garden. Consequently, every little heap of fallen leaves assumes the size and importance of a haystack. It will surprise you how much rubbish you find, for leaves constantly fall, soil is always spilling from containers or trickling out from the drainage holes, even airborne dust will collect on a wet floor or on damp foliage and accumulate until it is noticeable. Cleanliness is easily achieved if considered a constant aim and it amply repays the relatively few moments it takes.

If you have sufficient space it is possible to put these gleanings of garden rubbish to good use by making a rich compost from them. Keep a strong black plastic sack and tip everything except diseased plant tissue into this. Moisten this occasionally if it seems dry and at the quarter, half and three-quarters full levels add a handful of one of the compost accelerators. It may take up to a year, but in that time you will have accumulated a valuable source of good, rich compost all from your own garden rubbish.

Choosing Containers

Cleanliness is easier if your containers are chosen with care. Never attempt to economize by using, for example, old fruit trays or half broken boxes from the market to hold the soil in which your plants will grow. Not only will they look shabby and unkempt, they will spill soil and so expose roots. They will provide a snug home for insect pests until they disintegrate even further and finally collapse, to spread their contents on the ground.

On the other hand, there is no need to insist only on brand new or even purpose-built containers unless you wish to create a pleasant uniformity in your display, when you may be able to obtain a family range of containers all made of one material, all to one basic pattern, although preferably in several different shapes and sizes. This makes a unity of your garden and helps relegate the containers to the background and focus attention on the flowers and the foliage. However, it is equally possible to achieve attractive results by growing plants in a wide variety of interesting containers, as described later in this book (see pp 53–6).

There is no doubt that stone and terracotta are the ideal materials for plant containers, probably because both have an affinity with the soil from which they came in the first place. Both of these materials, then, would be ideal for a patio garden. On a balcony, however, and on a roof, these materials are generally too heavy to be practical. Apart from their dead weight while in position, they have to be transported to the site and then hoisted to upper levels before being installed in position.

Stone and terracotta containers almost invariably have efficient drainage holes in their bases, sometimes so large and so efficient that the soil they contain tends to get washed out when the plants are watered. So it is as well to minimize this possible disadvantage. This can be done in several ways. You can place a piece of coarse sacking in the base of the container before adding the soil. This will strain any exccess water as it flows away and prevent soil trickling through. The same can be done by slipping into the base and over the drainage hole or holes a small square of perforated metal; this gardening accessory can be bought from many garden centres. But the best method to adopt is to fill the base of the container to a level of at least 2.5cm (1in) and, if suitable, up to 6-8cm (2-3in) with broken flower pots, pebbles or any similar material that will allow water to pass freely but will retain the soil.

It can be helpful to have the necessary drainage holes not in

Some of the many attractive containers available. l. to r. *Large terracotta pot, stone urn, plastic tub, wooden half-barrel. Always choose containers to suit both the plants and the location: smaller or lightweight designs for balcony or roof; larger, heavier ones for patios.*

the base but in one of the sides, raised perhaps just 2-3cm (1in) from the base. The reason for this is that it creates a very small reservoir of water at the base of the container, and this will be just enough to keep the lower half of the compost a little moister than it would otherwise be. Few pots are made this way today, which is a pity, but it is perfectly possible to block the central drainage hole in the base with a wine cork and drill one or two holes in the side instead; or, if you are making your own containers, remember that this stratagem can prove useful. But bear one point in mind: do not make the little trough or reservoir too large or deep. If water hangs about in the base of a container for too long it can become stale and smelly. If this happens, water the container over-lavishly and allow the fresh water to flush out the old. In any case, among the materials in the drainage layer at the base of the pot you could include a few nuggets of charcoal, the kind used for a barbecue, and these will help to absorb any offensive smells.

There is another and highly important reason why drainage should be swift and efficient in all plant containers. Not only must the reservoir of soil be retained, but the rush of water through this soil when applied either from a can or hose should be unimpeded. We all know and appreciate that plants need watering and that plant roots in the container must therefore be given water at reasonable intervals. What is not so evident is that those roots also need air, a food just as important as water. When watering a plant in a flower pot or any other form of container, the moisture disappears through the soil and, if sufficient is given, it travels through the drainage hole or holes at the base. In so doing, it allows a supply of fresh air to follow, which displaces the stale air that has previously filled the innumerable crevices in the soil. This fresh air is important, hence the necessity of thorough watering and drainage.

A further consideration of importance regarding drainage concerns the question of whether or not the containers should be raised from the ground. If they are stood flat on the floor or paving, then drainage through the base is inhibited to some degree — not usually enough to be serious, but sufficient to merit further comment. If the base of the container stands on the floor, then water will still seep through but a residue will remain as a wet or damp patch immediately under the base. This can cause harm, both to the floor and to the container, and for this reason it is wise, where conditions are suitable, to raise the container slightly from the floor. Stand it on two or more blocks of wood, depending on its shape and size. Apart from aiding drainage, this will allow the portion of floor immediately beneath the container to dry out and it will make cleaning so much easier.

These comments on the importance of drainage apply

regardless of the type of container or the material from which it is made but have special relevance if the container is made of wood, which will rot more quickly and more easily if allowed to remain moist for long periods. As previously mentioned, stone or terracotta are ideal materials for containers at ground level on a patio but normally too heavy for balcony or roof. Here modern plastics come into their own, for these are lightweight, produced in a vast number of shapes, designs and colours, almost rot-proof (although they may tend to discolour or disintegrate after a considerable period in sunlight), some can be painted in different colours and all are usually washable so that city grime and dust can be removed.

Glass fibre is arguably the best of these lightweight materials; it is slightly more expensive but longer lasting and available in a number of colours and designs, some resembling antique lead. So many types of moulded plastic containers are available that it is impossible to generalize, except to advise that too light and too thin a material should not be chosen, nor one in a colour that is likely to grate on your nerves after a time. It is all very well after a bleak winter to plant daffodil bulbs in a bright yellow container and to enjoy the vivid colour through the dark days of early spring, but by next winter this yellow will have dulled, so it is best to choose your permanent containers in neutral colours and allow the plants themselves to brighten the scene.

Some plastic containers come without drainage holes in the base, largely because this enables them to be used indoors without fear of them damaging furnishings. Sometimes special places in the base are indicated where thinner material allows for drainage holes to be pierced easily. But whether or not these places are specially provided, it is a comparatively simple matter to make holes with a drill, a nail or even a red hot poker. Do not be stingy when making holes, bearing in mind that small holes become more easily blocked than large and that plenty of drainage allows a swift change of air within the soil or compost in the container.

Tools and Equipment

As we have seen, gardening in containers provides us with a number of advantages, but one which has not yet been mentioned is that we need very few of the expensive and space occupying tools that we would find essential for ground level gardening. We need no spades, no forks, no rakes or hoes, no wheelbarrows and perhaps, best of all, we need no lawn-mowers, no cultivators, no spreaders. A short length of hose can sometimes be helpful if our small scale garden is not too small, but under normal conditions a single watering can is all we will require for that job.

As tools will be kept to a minimum it is sensible to get the best. There are two perfectly practical reasons for this advice: high quality garden tools are made of strong materials which last well, are solid but not heavy and are easy to use. For example, a simple hand trowel can be bought cheaply enough, but it is likely to buckle in use, it can feel unbalanced and awkward, the metal will rust, the handle will come loose or will split. But a good quality tool will be made of stainless steel in a gauge heavy enough to stand up to any amount of rough handling. Apart from feel, appearance and balance in the hand, soil does not stick to a stainless steel tool and it is therefore both easier to use and to clean.

It will really be helpful to have two trowels rather than one, the first with a wide, flat blade and the second with one which is slimmer, more curved and pointed at the tip. All jobs needing to be done by these tools can then be carried out successfully. A hand fork of similar size, again of heavy gauge stainless steel, is also helpful, mainly for planting and for aerating the soil surface. Both the fork and trowels will normally be about 23–30cm (9–12in) long and weigh something like 225g (½ lb) each.

It will be useful, though not always essential, depending on the size and contents of your garden, to own a pair of secateurs. These will be used for comparatively light operations so it will be unnecessary to spend the considerable sum required to buy a first class pair. Buy some in the intermediate range, with a scissors cut rather than the blade and anvil type, for this way you get a cleaner cut on the soft plant materials. Keep these secateurs clean and oiled, for plant saps can gum up the blades and make them difficult and inefficient to operate.

A watering can is essential and should be chosen with care and with the answers to several important questions in mind. For instance, how far will it have to be carried from the nearest source of water? How important will it be to avoid spillages on the way? How strong are you? How near to the various containers can you stand when watering the plants? Where will you store the can when it is not in use? Will you use it only for watering — or also for applying fertilizers, fungicides and insecticides?

Although a plastic watering can will have a shorter life than a good metal one, it will weigh less and should give you less trouble in the long run. Try to store it away from sunlight, for ultra-violet light will lead to a gradual weakening and breakdown of the plastic. Get a can with a long spout if possible and with a rose that can quickly and easily be removed for cleaning. Watering cans are available in different sizes, but the most convenient and least tiring usually hold between 4.5 litres (1gal) and 9 litres (2 gal), with those of a capacity of about 6.8 litres (1½ gal) being probably the most popular. Remember that water weighs approximately 4.5kg (10lbs) per 4.5 litres (1 gal), so a full can can be a considerable weight if you have to carry it far or have to lean over or lift it up to carry out watering which requires great accuracy. So if your balcony, roof garden or patio is a bit larger than small scale and contains many plants you will save yourself a lot of strain, time and trouble if you install a hose pipe to speed your watering. Bear in mind also that it is human nature to avoid a task that involves considerable time or labour, and to prefer a task that consists of no more than turning a tap and then holding a hose end above a number of plant containers!

All the tools necessary for small scale gardening are displayed around the fatshedera in its traditional oak tub. l. to r. *Secateurs, broad and narrow trowels with hand fork, gardening apron and pruning knife, plastic watering can with rose spout and a small hand sprayer.*

There will be times when in all but the smallest of container gardens you will wish to spray your plants, perhaps with an insecticide to clear an infestation of greenfly, perhaps with a fungicide because of the possible onset of disease, perhaps with a foliar feed to encourage a spring burst of growth in laggardly plants. In all but really large container gardens you will find that a simple plastic pressure sprayer will be quite sufficient. These sprayers are not expensive and are foolproof so long as you keep them clean and empty when not in use. If you leave any garden chemical in them, or even plain water, for long periods, the filters will clog and cause an annoying and time wasting effort to clear them.

These are the only essential tools you will need for your small scale garden, although it may be advisable to duplicate one or two items, such as the watering can and perhaps the sprayer, so that you can have supplies of an insecticide and a fungicide to hand if required at the same time.

But an additional item mentioned earlier which is in many ways quite invaluable, will be a lightweight plastic bucket or plastic refuse sack, to be used mainly for the collection of dead leaves, for prunings, for the deposit of grime, grit or soil swept from the surface. If you merely collect together the rubbish gathered from various parts of the garden, intending to sweep it into a dustpan or other receptacle, by the time you have turned around much of it will have been dispersed again by the wind. A light plastic bucket or sack can be used constantly for everything, every tiny piece of waste, to make for a clean and disease-free garden.

A single-bladed penknife will be useful for pruning at certain times and a gardening apron, with a pocket to hold the penknife and secateurs, will make gardening easier and keep your clothes clean. This will be especially necessary for the small scale gardener who may not feel that the size of the garden merits special gardening clothes. Equally, it may be useful to have a pair of gardening gloves to wear when doing any dirty jobs or when handling prickly plants, such as roses.

Soils and Composts

Both soils and composts exist mainly to hold roots in place and to absorb and release to these roots the moisture, the plant foods and the air that are needed to promote healthy growth in a plant. A compost is generally understood to be a soil medium composed of additional materials such as peat, which can provide extra bulk and lightness to the soil; sand, which gives additional openness and aeration, so improving the drainage; and plant foods in the form of various chemical compounds.

Many small scale gardeners just do not have the facilities themselves to fill their plant containers with their own soil from their own gardens. To go out into a park or countryside and fill a sack with soil can be difficult and may be prohibited in some places, but fortunately there are ready-made soils of several different types for sale at garden centres, nurseries, seed and hardware stores and even some supermarkets. Some of these are even said to contain no soil. These last are peat-based composts carefully blended and balanced as a growing medium, incorporating plant foods and all the necessary ingredients for plant health. Others may have various proprietary names, but most are based on the familiar John Innes recipes formulated 50 years or more ago by the Horticultural Institution of that name. They consist of special proportions of sterilized garden loam, peat, sharp sand, lime and growth chemicals. They can be bought in small quantities in three strengths, for seedlings, for medium sized plants and for mature specimens, and there are also formulations for seed sowing, or without lime so that acid-loving plants can be grown.

Unfortunately, not all of these formulations are of the quality that they claim and it is possible to buy a bag only to find that it contains a piece of root, a stone or some other alien matter. The mixture is supposed to be sterilized so that any weed seeds it contains will be killed, yet occasionally mixtures produce a prolific crop of weeds when in use. The only practical answer to this problem is to try various branded products until you find one that appears to be best suited to the purpose you have in mind. Alternatively, make your own. This can be a somewhat lengthy process involving the cooking by some means or another of considerable quantities of soil and the addition of meticulously measured amounts of the correct type of peat, the correct type of sand, the correct chemicals, and the careful mixing together of these substances, a task generally to be urged only on the genuinely enthusiastic gardener. However, if you have the time and the enthusiasm to try your hand at making your own compost, the appropriate John Innes recipes are given in detail overleaf.

The Standard John Innes Potting Compost comprises:

7 parts by loose bulk loam (sterilized)

3 parts peat

2 parts sand

To this mixture is added 113.5g (4oz) of a chemical mix made up of 2 parts by weight hoof and horn meal, 2 parts superphosphate of lime and 1 part sulphate of potash. In addition 21.25g ($\frac{3}{4}$oz) of finely ground chalk or limestone per 3.64 litres (1 bushel) is also added. This is the basic mixture. For more mature plants, the fertilizer supplement can be doubled, and for fully grown trees and shrubs, trebled. These, then, are the J.I. Potting Composts Nos.1, 2 and 3.

The seed mixture (John Innes Seed Compost) is a little different, as might be expected. It is:

2 parts by loose bulk medium loam (sterilized)

1 part peat

1 part sand

And to each 36.4 litres (1 bushel) of this mixture is added 42.5g ($\frac{1}{2}$ oz) superphosphate of lime and 21.25g ($\frac{3}{4}$oz) finely ground chalk or limestone.

As mentioned, the loam should preferably be sterilized. It is possible to buy special heaters to do this which are expensive if only small quantities are required. In the latter case, a few handfuls of loam can be tied securely into a clean cloth and placed in a kitchen steamer for 20 minutes at 93.3°C (200°F).

Untreated garden soil is almost certainly of the wrong texture for container gardening. It is sure to contain vast numbers of dormant weed seeds just waiting to germinate. It almost certainly contains insect pests and disease spores. For these reasons it is inadvisable to use it without special treatment in the creation of a container garden. This said, if it is freely available and you are aware of its drawbacks, then it might be the answer to several problems. But give it greater porosity by adding to it up to a quarter of its bulk in sharp sand and another quarter in coarse peat. Lacking these, and cutting out still another step, leave out the sand and the peat and add instead rather less than a quarter, say an eighth, of perlite or horticultural vermiculite. The first consists of millions of little white bubbles or balls which serve to lighten the soil, improve its drainage and ability to absorb and retain moisture, while the second is a flaky mineral which does the same things.

The soil mixture you have made like this will be suitable for all plants except acid lovers and seed sowing. It is almost certain that weeds will appear on the soil surface after a period, but if the compost has been used as a base for a comparatively mature plant, then these will be easy enough to recognize and to pull out by hand. If disease is present it is unlikely to attack a mature plant and younger ones can be given a light fungicidal spray.

Whatever soil mixture or compost is used in small scale gardening, one should bear in mind that under certain circumstances, particularly on a balcony or roof garden, it will

A major benefit of container gardening is that purpose-made soil mixtures can be used to grow plants requiring different soils. Here, a rose bush flourishes in neutral soil and a rhododendron in a special acid compost.

tend to dry out at the top of the container and in a dry state will be light enough to be blown away. This can severely inconvenience neighbours and at the same time seriously reduce the amount of growing matter in the containers. To avoid this, and at the same time to help conserve the moisture content of the soil in the containers, it can be worthwhile to cover the surface with a heavier material which at the same time is attractive to the eye. Granite or marble chips are often used, simply spread lightly on the surface of the soil in the pots. Pea gravel, or even larger pebbles, will fulfil this function just as easily. This surface of heavier material will serve to hold down and secure the upper layers of soil; it will also act as a mulch or ground cover to discourage the growth of any weeds and the evaporation of moisture from the surface. It is a minor refinement, not a necessity, yet if you buy a small bag of granite chips and try a scattering on the surface of one of your containers, the chances are that the added attractiveness will so please you that you will want to use it on your other containers.

Before we leave the subject of soils and composts, it is worth mentioning some of the variations in soil requirements of certain different types of plants. In the first place, it will be obvious that to grow a tree or a mature shrub will require a pot or container deep enough to cover the sometimes considerable root system. At the same time, it must be appreciated that a comparatively large plant will have an adult appetite. In other words, the soil in which it grows should have sufficient fertilizer content to keep the stems, foliage and flowers of the plant in strong, growing health for the forseeable future. Similarly, smaller plants or seedlings will require fewer and less strong foodstuffs in their diet.

It is well known that certain plants, such as rhododendrons and many ericas, require a lime-free soil in which to grow and give of their best. Equally, other plants, such as dianthus, like a modicum of lime in their diet. One of the great advantages of container gardening is that both lime haters and lime lovers can be grown next to each other, an achievement impossible in the open ground of a garden. It is possible to buy acid or lime-free composts and alkaline composts, put them in separate containers and grow in them the plants most suited to their qualities. But bear one little matter in mind here: it is no good importing a special lime-free soil for your rhododendron tub if you are going to moisten it with tap water containing a high proportion of lime. Instead, collect rain water and use this.

Growbags

In some ways, the ultimate in convenience gardening arrived only a few years ago with the appearance of the growbag. As the name suggests, this is a conveniently large plastic bag or sack containing a specially prepared soil or compost, usually a peat mix, enriched with growth chemicals. Instead of tipping this mixture into a container, the sack is laid flat on the ground and a marked panel, or sometimes more than one, is cut away so that in effect the sack becomes a container. Some growbags come with the peat mixture dehydrated and consolidated into a lightweight board, requiring only the addition of water for it to swell into exactly the same growing medium as in other bags.

The plants, usually tomatoes, are planted in this mixture, the correct amount of water is added and the plants begin to grow. It's simple and convenient. It is also expensive, but on the other hand the compost in the sack is not wasted if it can be placed on the garden soil. And if no garden is available, then it can be added in small proportions to soils used in other containers. It is unwise to try to use it again and again as it stands, for not only will the major virtues of the soil have been used and absorbed by the plants it grew in the first place, but there is always the possibility that minor disease organisms may have built up, unimportant in small quantities but potentially harmful in large.

If you do decide to make use of a growbag for a second crop, add a handful of a balanced fertilizer and a little lime. The most successful second crops are usually lettuces, radishes and spring onions. Sow the seed in spring. Never attempt to follow one crop with another of the same kind.

Because these growbags are relatively expensive, it is wise to use them for special crops rather than waste their special benefits on plants which can equally well be grown anywhere else. Tomatoes have already been mentioned. It is possible to buy or make supports for use with growbags which will support tomato plants as they grow, but if the plants are large and heavy it is usually best to erect another separate structure something like a high jump frame, with strong and rigid supports at each end and a cane horizontal bar between the two. Vertical bamboo canes reach upwards from the plants to this horizontal bar where they are tied in place.

But tomatoes are not the only suitable first crop. Lettuces or aubergines can also be grown and, whatever the main crop, it is always possible to slip in a few seeds of a catch crop, such as radishes, which will occupy little space, will grow quickly and can be removed and eaten almost within a matter of days.

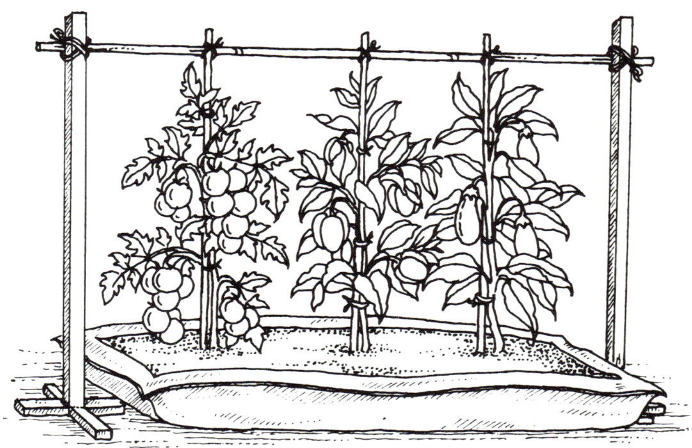

You can easily make this simple but efficient support for growbag food crops (here l. to r. *tomatoes, peppers and aubergines). Wooden side supports have a cane crossbar tied to them: the three canes supporting the plants are tied to this crossbar, which can be adjusted to suit the height of the plants.*

Growbags are of use only in spring and summer in the open. Heavy winter rains, snows and frosts will fill them with water or otherwise cause drainage problems. If too much water gets into the bags the compost will overflow and cause problems. But in spite of the fact that the season for using growbags is limited, much use can be made of them and because they are comparatively expensive it is only right that they should produce crops with a leaning towards luxury. Apart from tomatoes, aubergines, lettuce, radishes and spring onions, strawberries will grow equally well. Cucumbers and all the varieties of squashes can be grown successfully. The many kinds of herbs grow well to delight the gourmet. It is not usually advisable to grow root crops, because the bags are normally too shallow for this purpose. On the other hand, I know of one keen gardener who has grown small annual crops of early potatoes in growbags and swears that they are the best his family have ever tasted!

Small Scale Gardening
PART II

MAKING THE MOST OF YOUR SPACE

♦

It is probably true to say that most small scale gardening is carried out in towns and cities, where space is limited and many buildings have no ground level gardens. One of the problems about growing plants in cities is the quality of the light. We can all accept the limitations imposed by the shadow of a nearby building or an adjoining wall and do our best to work within these restrictions. Less easy to accept is the overall, pervading low grade of light. This is due to the amount of dust in the air from ground level sometimes up to the clouds, and it means that the sum total of light available to plants may in some cases be too little to permit proper growth, but the situation is improving with increasingly efficient pollution control in cities.

Light is of vital importance to plants and without it they will not grow. Light is the source of the energy needed by the plant to manufacture sugars and oxygen from the carbon dioxide of the atmosphere and the water from its roots — the process known as photosynthesis. Where light is poor, plants will be a pale green in colour, limp, weak, thin and unproductive, stems and foliage being sappy and almost wet simply because there is insufficient energy to promote a healthy giving off of oxygen, known as transpiration.

Sometimes, however, it is possible to provide additional artificial light. It is worth noting that trees and shrubs nearest to street lights in cities always seem to grow best, flower earlier and more abundantly than those planted further away from this light. So plants grown on a balcony or patio can gain some benefit from the light shining through an uncurtained window, for instance, and it will always be helpful to take

The ideal patio is sunny and protected. Herbs can be grown in a window box, tomatoes in a growbag, strawberries in a barrel and a small apple tree in a tub, as well as a profusion of flowering plants, including pendant fuchsias and begonias, trailing lobelia, lilies, nicotiana (tobacco plants) and miniature plants in a sink garden.

advantage of this. Further ideas on how to increase light are suggested later on when advice is given on planting in a shady area (see pp 34–7).

Planting in a Sunny Position

The gardener with a sunny small scale garden will, of course, have plenty of necessary light, but there are still some drawbacks to contend with. Nearly all plants growing in a garden get some degree of protection from their neighbours, protection from wind, rain and snow — and from the sun. At the same time, their roots are growing deep into the cool, rich , moist earth of the garden. But the plant growing in a container on a patio, balcony or roof gets much less protection from its neighbours, its container is also sunwarmed, the floor on which it stands reflects the heat of the sun — and the very walls of the buildings in the immediate vicinity absorb and then release more warmth.

There are some plants which revel in this heat, but the majority find it too much and sometimes curl up and die. The answer, of course, is to choose plants carefully which are to be grown in full sun, and a variety of plants most suited to sunny situations is included among the plants described in the final section of this book. But in addition to this, it is quite possible with very little trouble to install or provide various protective devices which will reduce the strength of the heat from the sun without appreciably reducing the light.

By taking note of the position of the sun at different times of the day and at different seasons it is easy to discover the spots most exposed to long periods of baking heat. You can then keep the more delicate plants out of these spots, moving them so that the sun will strike them only for brief periods. Alternatively, it may be possible to leave these delicate plants in their usual positions and to move certain other plants so that these receive the full force of the sun and protect their delicate neighbours with their shade. It may be necessary to lift some of these plants onto an upturned flower pot or a block of wood to provide the necessary shade. These are fairly simple matters requiring only a little observation and ingenuity. In addition, it might be possible to install a canvas curtain or screen which can be pulled or positioned on sunny days and left unused on others.

By all means water plants copiously before the sun reaches its position of greatest strength and, if possible, also water the floor and even the walls. But on no account allow drops of water to remain on leaves or flowers when the sun is strong, for each drop will act as a magnifying glass and brown burn marks may be left.

Planting in a Shady Area

It is easier to reduce the amount of light reaching a certain area than to increase it, so shade planting is more difficult than planting to avoid too much sun. Certainly, the first thing to do, once again, is to look carefully at the site to decide whether any moving about of plants will provide more light for those that need it. Taller, heavier, darker plants can be moved to allow light through to smaller, more delicate subjects, and those plants that require the most light should be positioned so that they get it. A general rule to remember is that the darker green and heavier the plant leaf, the less light it will need.

Certain plants, most ferns for example, actively dislike direct sun and grow well in shade so long as their roots are kept moist. This is evident from the number of ferns seen growing wild in the cracks of a wall or the guttering of an empty building in the centre of a city. The great variety of their foliage is what makes them attractive plants to grow in a shady area. Some have delicate fronds, others thicker leaves in interesting shapes. Popular ferns are illustrated in the final section of the book on plants for the small scale garden (see p 119), together with a selection of other flowering and foliage plants suitable for growing in shade.

Many varieties of conifer and ivy will grow in full or partial shade; ivy is especially useful for disguising ugly pipes on the walls of basement patios, as it can be trained to grow up them. Conifers and ivies are, of course, evergreen, which is an asset during dark winter days. In spring and summer, however, what is most needed in a shady site is the brightness and cheerfulness of flowers, since ferns, ivies and conifers do not flower. This can be achieved. In spring, snowdrops will grow in pretty groups in containers in full or partial shade and daffodils, too, will tolerate partial shade. Trailing nasturtiums and Iceland poppies can usually be relied on to make a colourful

The buildings, walls and fences that bring shade to a patio also protect it from strong winds Climbers such as honeysuckle, clematis and ivies will grow undisturbed, ferns will flourish in the shade and a hydrangea gains because its soil will not dry out so quickly as it would in the sun.

summer display in a window box, hanging basket or tub where there is little sunshine. Pansies do not like strong sunlight and *Viola labradorica purpurea* is particularly good for shady positions, with its pretty purplish leaves and pink flowers. Unlike ferns, it prefers a well-drained soil. *Viola wittrockiana* is the type of pansy with the black markings on shades of purple, blue, red, white and yellow; it will grow in partial shade. Forget-me-nots (*Myosotis sylvatica*) and *Lobelia erinus* will grow in shade. The delightful blue flowers of the African lily and the white, purple, blue or pink flowers of campanula varieties all add colour and interest to a partially shady site.

The twining, climbing varieties of honeysuckle also do well in partial shade and bring the bonus of their lovely scent. Clematis likes to have its roots in shade and will flower in partial shade. Surprisingly, some climbing and rambling roses will grow in shade, such as New Dawn and Sanders White.

It is certainly worth mentioning that unusual containers can come into their own in a shady site, adding both character and colour. The old terracotta chimney illustrated on page 56, which has trailing ivy growing from a pot fixed in the top, would look charmingly mellow in a shady corner – and the interesting coal-hod container shown on page 110, planted with trailing nasturtiums, would also be a very attractive feature.

At this point, it might be useful to advocate a little light relief, in two senses of the phrase, by suggesting that there is nothing wrong with introducing artificial objects onto a balcony, roof garden or patio. Have you a little statuette or some other colourful and amusing object that would bring some brightness to the scene? Take a good look at the surroundings. Are the walls dark and dingy? Need they be? Can they be painted, either white or some other attractive light colour? This would reflect a surprising amount of light into what might otherwise be a very dark corner. Could you even paint a colourful mural? Is there a position where an old mirror could be placed to reflect light into a dark area? Can you put down some white tiles on the floor? Not to cover the entire space but just certain areas where the light is most murky.

All of these artifices are legitimate and helpful. After all, it's your garden space and you can do with it what you will! Bear in mind that everything you do to improve a shady small scale garden will reward you, both in terms of its appearance and the pleasure you will gain from seeing your plants do well.

Small Scale Gardening
PART III

WINDOW BOXES, HANGING BASKETS AND IMPROVISATIONS

♦

For those who live in flats or apartments without gardens, balconies or a flat roof, almost the only place for any outdoor gardening is in a window box, or series of window boxes. A window box can either sit on the window ledge or be secured to the wall below a window, and is tended from indoors. The most attractive are filled with flowering plants which can be seen and enjoyed from both inside and outside the building.

Sometimes byelaws or leasehold conditions prohibit or set limits to the installation of window boxes and so it is sensible to check if you have any doubts on this. It is also essential to make quite sure of the condition of window sills or ledges and the strength of window frames and exterior walls. It is quite possible for frames to rot, ledges to crumble and mortar between bricks to deteriorate without these defects being noticeable except under close examination. Remember that your window box is entirely your responsibility.

Fitting a Window Box

A window box which is secured below a window is in some ways preferable to one which sits on the sill, since it does not obstruct light and is easier to look after. However, the most important thing is to ensure that it is well secured so that it cannot cause damage or harm to people or property below. Always bear in mind that a window box can be bulky and heavy enough to kill a passer-by if it falls, or cause considerable damage to a vehicle. If the box stands on a window ledge, secure it with brackets to the side walls or with chain supports to the walls on each side. If it hangs beneath, have special supports made which are securely screwed to the face of the building. It must be fixed so that opening the window cannot disturb it, no amount of wind can dislodge it and the planting and tending of it leaves it safe and secure.

One of the best ways of securing an attractive window box to a ledge is to make an open frame or basket into which the box will fit. This frame should be securely fixed to the window frame at the base and sides, it should be strongly made and reinforced inside with metal corner struts. The window box it will hold will have to be slightly smaller than would otherwise be necessary, but it can be of much lighter construction and material.

Window boxes are available in cement, terracotta, stone, wood or plastic, and some consist of no more than a wire or metal frame which holds a number of plastic or earthenware flowerpots in position. Wood is the most popular material because it can easily be used to make a box suitable for a particular site.

Choose a hardwood such as oak or elm rather than a softwood such as pine, because the latter will soon rot with the constant contact with moist soil. It should be no less than 2cm (¾in) thick and the box should be stoutly made with adequate bracing, using galvanized or brass screws. Dimensions must obviously vary, depending on the site, but no window box

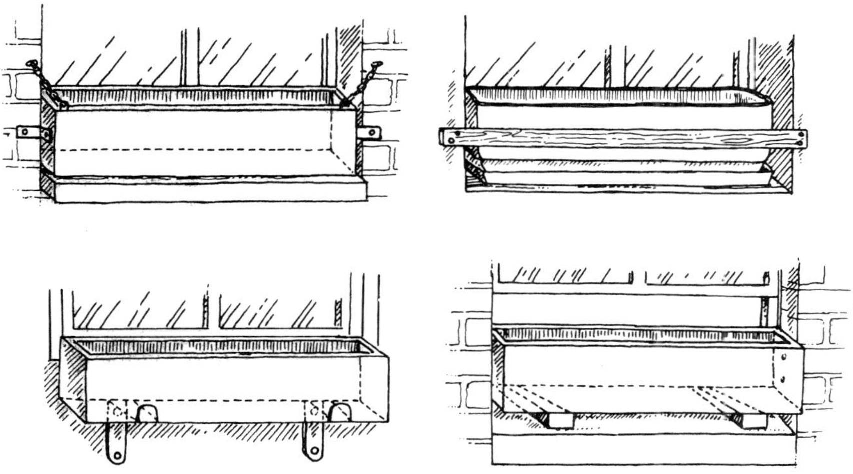

Four ways of fitting a window box. Top l. *The box is secured to the walls on either side by brackets and chain supports.* Lower l. *To fit a box where there is no window-sill, use strong bracket supports below window level and also chain supports, as above, if necessary.* Top r. *A wooden or metal guard rail in front of the box holds it safely in place and allows it to be moved so that the drip tray can be emptied.* Lower r. *Tapered wooden blocks secure a box on a sloping or uneven window-sill; screws hold it to the side walls. A drip tray can be placed under the box between the blocks.*

should be less than 15cm (6in) deep. There should be wedges for lifting the floor of the box slightly from the window-sill to aid drainage.

Paint the finished box inside and out with two coats of a non-toxic staining wood preservative and then finish the outside with two coats of polyurethane. Or you can use ordinary paint; first apply a primer, then an undercoat followed by two topcoats. Do this before the box is placed in position, remembering also to preserve and conceal the supports with paint. Be sure to make adequate provision for drainage by drilling at least two holes in the base of each window box before it is secured in position, as shown on the previous page.

It is sensible to try to ensure that excess water trickling through during the watering of plants can be caught or interrupted so as not to fall on the face of the building or on the

Planted in autumn to flower in spring – a brilliant display of dwarf tulips, hyacinths and primulas offset by trailing ivy, the permanent feature of the box.

ground or people beneath. The best solution is to fit a drip tray which can be removed and emptied after each watering (and after heavy rain), but it is sometimes either impossible to fit one or too difficult to move it when full. It is then necessary to water with great care. Choose a time of day when it is unlikely that people will be walking underneath or be sure to water only a little at a time so that virtually no water escapes through the drainage holes in the base of the window box.

Window Box Gardening

Never try to fill a window box before it is placed in position; it will be heavy enough to move and fix in place without the addition of drainage material and soil. When it is securely in place in or below the window space, put a layer of broken crocks or similar material at least 2.5 cm (lin) deep in the base, covering the drainage holes so that soil does not trickle through. On top of this drainage layer you can place a sheet of heavy black plastic, which can be cut from a bag which contained peat. This should first be punctured in several places to allow water to trickle through and it should be just a little larger than the floor of the box so that when in position the plastic will rise for 2-3cm (lin) up the sides of the box. This will also help to prevent soil from trickling through the drainage holes and, more

A colourful summer window box planted with petunias, Marguerite daisies and ageratum, complemented by the vivid coleus foliage.

important, will stop any plant roots from forcing their way out of the box through the drainage holes.

Finally, fill the box with the required soil mixture (see pp 22–7), allowing space at the top both for planting and for watering. When planting, remember that the soil will be comparatively loose, so firm it around the plant roots securely. Water-in well and regularly ensure that the soil is kept moist for the first week or two, as it can take a little while for the whole of the box to become uniformly moist.

There is, of course, no reason why window box plants should be grown in the soil. Instead, they can remain in their own pots and either be placed inside the box for protection and concealment or have their pots 'plunged' to rim level in the box soil. The second method is preferable to the first because the pots will retain their moisture for a longer period. But the main advantage of organizing a display in this way is that each plant can be instantly removed and replaced when it is no longer at its best. It needs merely to be lifted from the box and replaced with another pot containing a more attractive plant.

If plants in these pots are well grown, thick, lush and with plenty of flowers, they will merge together above the rim of the box and it will be impossible to tell that they are in fact growing in a series of separate containers. But if they are small and sparse, too young and immature to be worthy of display, they will take some time before they do you credit, unless the spaces between the pots are filled with some more permanent specimen plants.

This is really one of the most effective ways of maintaining a constant display, regardless of season. The window box should be planted up with a few subjects such as ivy, which will trail prettily down the front of the box and maintain its foliage throughout the year. If and when it grows too rampant it can easily and quickly be cut back to more manageable size without coming to any harm. The back half of the box can be decorated with one or more varieties of heather and another evergreen perennial; these will fill space, provide a constant green with

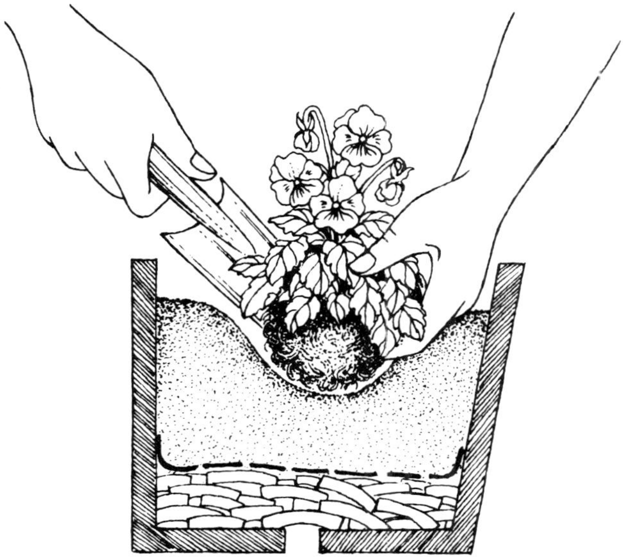

Mid-spring pansies coming into flower are planted in standard potting compost. The layer of pierced plastic prevents roots from growing through the drainage holes and soil escaping. The layer of pottery shards beneath ensures proper drainage.

occasional flower colour and not dominate the box in opposition to the more colourful and temporary annual or biennial flowers which will be grown in the middle and front of the box.

As a general rule, it is inadvisable to plant tall specimens in window boxes, other than certain climbers which can be supported and kept in place by wall ties or hooks. The reason is simply that winds can be too strong and the plants will become damaged, their flower heads torn off, their stems shattered. The only real exceptions are sturdy, firm and well anchored conifers. Dwarf forms can be strong enough to stand against winds, the foliage is securely anchored and there is little whip in the main trunk, so these can give some strength and solidity to the container.

In winter a subtle combination of ivies, heathers and a dwarf conifer will withstand harsh weather and show that nature is still very much alive.

Bulbs, corms and tubers — usually referred to collectively as bulbs — form the basis of one of the best possible groups of flowers for window box gardening. All are delightful and colourful and most are comparatively dwarf so that they can come to little harm in a gale. Bulbs differ from other plant structures in that the embryo plant, complete with tiny flower, is packed with its own food supply around it in a convenient, self-contained package; given the growing environment of soil and moisture, it is certain to develop into a mature and gorgeously flowered plant which will add colour and interest to your window box year after year.

There is no reason why a window box should be filled entirely with tulips or hyacinths. A mixture can perfectly well be made and many bulbs can be planted in the one box. But there are one or two points which should be watched. Make sure that flowering times fit in with your own programmes. Make sure that colours blend or contrast as you wish them to do and that shapes and textures conform to your plans. Some bulbs can be left in the boxes to flower again next year after the flower heads have been removed to prevent the formation of seed.

After they have flowered and their seed cases have been removed, most bulbs should be allowed to die down quietly in position, their fading foliage absorbing plant foods from the atmosphere and storing them in the bulb, ready to be awakened into growth and flower in the next season. This withering foliage can have a depressing and untidy appearance and it is best to remove the bulbs from the window box. They should then be roughly planted in garden soil, even in a box if necessary, until they have died down completely; the bulbs can then be removed, dried, cleaned and stored in a cool, dry place for planting in the next autumn so that they can become established before their flowering season.

When talking about bulbs and bulb flowers one tends to concentrate on the spring flowering kinds that bring such solace after the long, hard winter: daffodils, tulips and hyacinths, as well as tiny snowdrops and colourful crocuses. But there are many lovely summer and autumn flowering bulbs which are normally planted in spring — and because many of these are small they are well suited to a window box. Yet even some of the taller growing types can be grown successfully because their season is a time when strong, lashing winds and heavy, prolonged rains are not as prevalent as they are in winter. Some of the smaller examples include the little white crocus-like zephyranthes, autumn flowering crocuses and the colchicums. Sparaxis, tritonia and tigrida are all dainty and flowering when the majority of the summer blooms have gone and we begin to steel ourselves for the winter. Larger but still manageable plants include some of the smaller dahlias so vividly coloured, nerines, agapanthus and even some of the dwarfer gladioli, together with the similar and sweetly perfumed acidanthera.

These and the more normal range of herbaceous plants suitable for window boxes are discussed in greater detail in the section on plants at the end of this book and selections can be worked out from the suggestions made there.

Hanging Baskets

When we come to hanging baskets we enter a special and quite distinctive world of plant display. Considering the number of plants one sees that are grown in pots one can understand that there is only a minor difference between this and growing them in a window box or other container. But we take an outrageous step when we try to grow them in almost no soil and in a position where we normally see them not from above but from below! How, then, do we grow plants in this extraordinary manner and what types of plants should we choose?

It is possible to buy hanging baskets already planted up and ready to be hung in your own space, and if you see them for sale you might be advised to make a quick purchase for the following reasons. Hanging baskets are fiddly and time-consuming to prepare. They demand a surprising amount of growing material which must be at exactly the right stage of maturity, not yet at its magnificent best but past the gangling, immature stage. Because of these two reasons those who actually make and sell hanging baskets are almost always highly expert gardeners who not only know exactly what they are doing, but actually enjoy facing and overcoming all the problems. Hence those hanging baskets you see in nurseries or occasionally in florist shops are almost without exception magnificent and gorgeous, but you will find that they are probably sold already. The answer is to place a firm order this year for the hanging basket you would like to have next spring.

Planting a Hanging Basket

To be really effective, a hanging basket must be full of colour and appear to be almost a ball of flowers. Vivid pendant fuchsias and the luxuriant blooms of begonias make good basic ingredients, together with less exuberant flowers such as lobelia and forget-me-nots.

Few ways of displaying flowering or non-flowering plants are as attractive as in a hanging basket, yet few things can look worse than a basket that contains a straw coloured, untidy tangle of dead stems. There are one or two matters of technique and handling which should be appreciated and followed if the actual designing and planting of your own hanging baskets is to be attempted.

Hanging baskets usually come in the form of a half globe of heavy-gauge galvanized wire mesh with three or four suspension chains attached, leading to a heavy ring or hook which will carry the weight of the basket. Several different sizes are available. When choosing, bear in mind that the finished basket filled with plants and moist soil will be very heavy, so make sure that it can be lifted safely into position. Remember too that when planted up and growing well the overall dimensions will be roughly double those when the basket is empty, so allow plenty of space around and below the basket when it is in place. If it is too close to a wall it will rub in any wind and both damage the plants and stain the wall. If it is too low it may brush the heads of any people who have to walk beneath it. Make quite sure that the bracket which will carry the basket is strong enough to do so, that it is securely fixed to the wall and that the wall itself is strong enough to hold the bracket that holds the basket that holds the plants! Fixing a hanging basket securely is particularly important in a place where people will be walking under it, such as a porch.

Before starting to fill the basket, secure it so that it will not roll about on its spherical base. Take a bucket and stand it in the mouth of this. The traditional lining for a hanging basket is sphagnum moss. Handfulls of this are pressed into place around the whole of the interior to a thickness of 2-3cm (lin). This prevents the soil falling through, it absorbs moisture efficiently and it has a pleasant, neutral appearance. It also allows shoots and roots to grow through it with only minimal resistance.

But sphagnum moss is not always easily obtainable today, which is one reason why hanging baskets are now available in green plastic-covered mesh, with a fairly inconspicuous saucer at the base which will hold a reservoir of water and prevent soil dripping through.

Less effective than a sphagnum lining is one of plastic sheeting, but this does provide a compromise. Pierce a few small holes or slits in a piece of heavy grade black plastic sheeting, which has been cut to measure, and place this in the interior of the mesh half-sphere. When soil is added the plastic will be pressed against the mesh and will take its form. The

(a)

(b)

Planting a hanging basket. Place it in the top of a bucket (a) to hold it steady; line the interior with a layer of sphagnum moss.
Place a piece of plastic sheeting on this, slit in places to allow drainage (b). This can be used as a lining without sphagnum moss, if it is difficult to obtain.
Fill with a clay soil mixture (c), as this preserves moisture.
Set trailing plants, such as ivies and lobelia, at the sides (d) and the more upright ones in the centre (e), firming them in with more soil. Plants should spill over the sides, creating a mass of flowers and foliage.

(c)

(d)

(e)

little holes or slits are both to allow drainage and to permit little roots or shoots to be slipped into the soil from outside, so that stems will grow and trail attractively not only at the top but all around and below the basket. Use plants the same way, of course, with the sphagnum lined basket and the type with the saucer. Aim to make a complete ball of flowering growth.

It is easiest to fill as you plant. Arrange the lowest level of plants with their roots lying on the soil surface of the partially filled basket and their upper parts outside the basket. Cover the roots with soil and fill up to the height of the next layer and so on, finishing with the surface covering plants. A heavy or clay soil mixture is the best one to choose. This is simply because the greatest danger to plants in a hanging basket is that they dry out too quickly at the roots. The soil supply is relatively meagre, the basket is up in the air where it dries out quickly, it is largely out of sight and so out of mind and, finally, it is comparatively difficult to water. So the plants can easily wither and die.

It is therefore essential to make arrangements for watering hanging baskets simply and effectively and it is equally essential to establish a regular routine of watering so that it is never forgotten. Baskets can need water up to three or four times a day, depending on their location, their size and their contents. This can be a difficult and annoying chore if it is necessary to lift a heavy watering can above your head. There are two answers to this problem. Firstly, it may be possible to fit the basket to a rope and pulley so that it can be lowered easily for watering and tending and then hoisted back into place again. Another answer is to have ready a stout pole of some convenient length and some elastic bands or similar means of attaching a hose to the pole. It is then fairly easy to lift the pole up beside the hanging basket and direct a gentle jet of water into the basin.

Because a hanging basket is normally viewed from below, it is prettiest to fill it with cascading and trailing plants. Among these are ivy leaved pelargoniums, pendant fuchias, petunias, begonias, campanulas, calceolarias, nepeta, glecoma, thunbergia, nasturtiums, canary creeper, annual phlox, verbena, lobelia, impatiens and many more, some best for sun, some for shade. There are also a number of foliage plants. See the section at the end for further information.

Improvisations and Novelties

Although they are charming and dainty additions to the small scale garden, window boxes and hanging baskets have their limitations. The necessarily small size and shallow soil depth means that the range of plants they hold must be comparatively small and problems about watering and general maintenance may lead enthusiasts to look for other answers to

A wicker basket charmingly planted with fragrant, sun-loving lavender and pinks. Line it with plastic or foil to prevent the soil drying out too quickly.

their decorative ambitions. Fortunately there are many of these.

One of the simplest is the wall pot. This is no more than a container with a flat back which is hung on an outer wall. Usually made of terracotta or plastic, there are many shapes and sizes available. Their advantage is largely that the major problems of tending are simplified, for they are normally within reach from the floor or ground, although there is no reason why they should not be higher. Because they are pots and not baskets they can hold more soil for the plant or plants they are to contain. They do not normally have drainage holes, because drips would have to trickle down the wall surface and possibly cause staining.

This lack of drainage means that care must be taken when moistening the plant roots, for although all contained plants outdoors dry out quickly they must never be subjected to waterlogging or drowning. The answer is to make sure that the base of the container is covered with sufficient drainage material — broken crocks, pebbles and the like — to act as a reservoir, collecting and holding water and releasing it slowly to the soil when needed. Some wall vases or wall pots come with an integral water reservoir containing a small circle of clear plastic through which the level of the water can be seen. This is very helpful and these containers are not expensive.

As mentioned earlier (see pp 14–15), containers which stand on the ground do not have to be purpose-made. They can be improvised from anything decorative that will hold one or more plants, provided it is more or less watertight (with or without drainage holes), can be moved about easily and will withstand bad weather. The kitchen is a great source of novelty containers — saucepans, kettles, soup tureens and even a large teapot can be successfully used. Make sure you place a good layer of broken crocks and pebbles in the base, particularly if there are no drainage holes. If a container looks as though it might rust after a period out of doors, paint or otherwise rustproof it if possible. Do not use any material that is liable to disintegrate in poor weather, material such as papier mâché, from which some decorative boxes are made.

It may be possible to create a sense of decorative unity by arranging a family of related containers; for example, a range of different sizes of saucepans of the same colour or design. Or you could use a tiered attractively painted saucepan rack to stand one container above another to make a pillar of plants. Where space exists, an engaging feature can be constructed from a series of different sizes of old car tyres cut in half and painted some bright colour. A pyramid, spire or tower of flowers can be made by filling the largest half tyre with soil, placing the next size on it so that it rests on the curved inner edge of the larger tyre and then filling that with soil, and doing the same with the next size, until you have built your supply of tyres into as many pyramids as you want. Then flowers can be planted in each layer to achieve a tiered effect. Old tyres can frequently be had for the taking away from garages or tyre merchants.

Old chimney pots can often be found in builders' yards and sometimes in antique shops. A plant pot or other container should be placed in the top so that the actual chimney becomes more or less a pedestal. Most of these chimneys are of earthenware or terracotta, some in interesting decorative patterns. They may need repairing, but this can usually be done so that even the repair itself can contribute to the careless rhapsody of the display. An old wheelbarrow, particularly one of the traditional wooden kind, can make a fascinating and beautiful plant container which has the added quality of being perfect for its new task. If you have to use a modern metal wheelbarrow, give it a coat of paint to smarten it.

Some containers may require a lining before they can be used. A wicker basket, for example, can look pleasant indeed as the centre or highlight of a display, but any soil in it will dry out too quickly for it to be viable as a living plant container. It can be lined with plastic or even a material such as kitchen foil to render it waterproof certainly for a few months.

Ivy trails and twists with natural elegance from a pot fixed in the top of a mellow old terracotta chimney.

But containers need not have their plants actually growing in their soil. The plants can be in pots, merely placed in a decorative container and taken out and replaced as they fade, just as you might do in a window box. Much will depend on how easily you can obtain new plants and perhaps also on the occasion, for special displays of this kind can offer a gracious welcome to guests on a social occasion.

Sink Gardens

Sink gardens are much admired and can look antique, peaceful and tastefully attractive when planted with such items as house leeks, ferns, succulents, one or two dwarf conifers and a few selected dwarf specimens. Unfortunately, real stone sinks and troughs are now either impossible to find or available only at astronomic prices. Some are available in reconstituted stone and after a period in the open it is sometimes difficult to see that these are modern. It is also possible at comparatively little cost in money, materials or time to make your own stone sink that will compare very favourably with the genuine specimen and will, with reasonable care, last a number of years. I have two which I made myself more than 10 years ago and these now look even more like the real thing than at the beginning, with the moss and algae that have grown on them.

It is possible to make a sink using cement or concrete as the only material, but unless you have some knowledge of handling these materials and some experience of the reinforcement and bracing required, it is far better to stick to the easier and more foolproof method of making your own sink on the frame of a previous model. Many builders' yards contain battered old kitchen sinks made of glazed eathenware or porcelain, useless

Pretty and peaceful – a sink garden planted with sedums, sempervivums and saxifrages creates a restful theme in soft colours.

today for any purpose and hence usually available either free or at a very reasonable price. They are heavy and should be handled with care lest they fall and break. Mere cracks or chips will be unimportant.

When you get the old sink home, first decide where you intend to place it once completed and filled with plants, for it will be too heavy to move later. When you have selected its location, lift it onto a couple of bricks or some similar support to keep it clear of the ground and to assist drainage. It is helpful to slope the sink very slightly towards the interior drainage hole which will already exist. No other drainage hole will then be necessary.

The idea is to coat the white or yellow shining porcelain or earthenware with a material which will resemble stone. This coating is made of sand, cement and fine peat in the proportions of 1:1:2. By increasing slightly the amount of sand you get a somewhat yellower finish more like sandstone; to get a result more like limestone add a little more cement. Mix these ingredients together thoroughly while dry and then add water slowly and carefully until it holds together well and is in no way wet or runny.

Before applying the mixture to the shabby old sink, its surface will have to be treated with a bonding agent, of which there are many types available, used for fixing fabrics, floor tiles and the like. Spread this over the exterior walls making sure that every portion is covered fairly thickly. Take it over the rim and down into the interior walls a little way to just below the level where the soil will stop when the sink is filled. Again, take it down to the base on the exterior to where its finishing edge cannot be seen. Allow this bonding mixture to become tacky, almost dry, before applying the cement mixture.

The only effective way of applying this is by hand. If your skin is sensitive, use thick rubber gloves. Pick up a handful of the moist, pudding-like cement and peat mixture and press it firmly onto the tacky surface of the sink, covering it to depth of about 1cm (½in). You will find that quantities fall to the ground, so it will be helpful if you spread a plastic sheet below the sides of the sink to collect the excess, which can then be used again.

Do not try to smooth the surface as it is applied. Your finger marks when the material dries will look rather like the marks of a chisel. Instead, pat the soft mixture firmly into place, going over the entire surface to make sure that there are no bare patches or places where the cement is too thick or too thin. When the whole sink has been covered to your satisfaction, drape a wet sack or cloth over it and allow it to dry very slowly as this aids the adhesion and strengthens the coating mixture.

When it has dried completely, place one or two flat stones over the drainage hole and pour a good layer, not less than 2-3cm (1in) of drainage materials (broken crocks and pebbles) into the base before filling with your planting mixture, say John Innes Compost No. 2 (see pp 23–4). You can landscape your sink garden by the addition of a few rocks, either natural or made from your sand, cement and peat mixture, in which case the 'rock' will match the 'stone' of the container.

When planting, remember that your plants will have to be in proportion to the overall size of the sink, not only when newly planted, but when grown to mature size. So choose both small and slow growing plants, preferably those with tiny leaves. Sedums and stonecrops look well, as do some of the creeping thymes and saxifrages. If you wish to plant a tree, choose a dwarf, slow growing conifer.

When the planting has been completed, give your sink garden an attractive finish by covering the surface of the soil completely with a layer of granite chippings. Keep the soil slightly dry.

Small Scale Gardening
PART IV

LOOKING AFTER YOUR PLANTS

♦

It is probably true to say that most plants for the small scale garden are bought in a garden centre, market, seedman's shop or sometimes in a supermarket, rather than raised from seeds or cuttings by the gardener. It is probably also true to say that at least half of those plants sold are of such poor quality that they cannot hope to survive long after planting. There are a number of reasons for this. The market growers cannot normally be blamed, for if they produce poor quality plants they will not remain in business for long. But once the plants are out of their hands they can begin to suffer: they may not receive proper protection from the weather; they may not be watered when necessary; they may be knocked about in transit; they may be subjected to draughts or fumes; or they may merely hang about for days awaiting a buyer and become weak and weary in the process. Perhaps, though, the enthusiasm of the gardener can be almost as great a hazard.

Buying and Planting

Never buy tender young plants too early in the season. Time after time, year after year, gardeners are caught and intoxicated by a lovely spring day. They dash to shops or markets and come home laden with boxes of bedding plants which they eagerly plant out – only to find them all dead the next day because of a bitter night frost. You must therefore make sure that all danger of frost has passed before you spend money on tender young plants.

At this point, however, it should be mentioned that the most effective way of avoiding the misfortunes just mentioned is to grow your own plants from seed; this is not difficult so long as you have certain limited facilities, as described in the section on raising your own plants (see pp 86–93). But if buying your plants is the only option open to you, the cheapest way to obtain the usual spring bedding plants – the petunias, impatiens, lobelia and the like – which do so much to brighten and glorify window boxes and containers, is to go to a street market and look for trays or boxes of young plants.

Rather more expensive, but with less risk of loss through carelessness or weather, are more mature plants which are sold either in boxes or individual pots. These larger plants can be examined more easily. They should be ready to plant out in your containers, with their flower buds about to open, and looking as if they will grow into good, strong plants that will give lasting pleasure. So when you do buy, take care and examine every plant closely. Any which have dropped leaves on the soil or on the sides of the pot or box should be rejected, even though they may be offered as bargains. Never buy a plant with leaves which are flaccid, drooping, dried or wrinkled, or which are turning yellow. If any leaves look as if they have been nibbled or have holes in them there is likely to be a snail, a slug or perhaps earwigs or woodlice in the box or pot. Look carefully under the leaves and into the leaf joints or axils to make sure there are no greenfly. Reject any plant with any trace of mould on its leaves or stem.

A pot or box should be heavy, as this shows that it has been

(a)

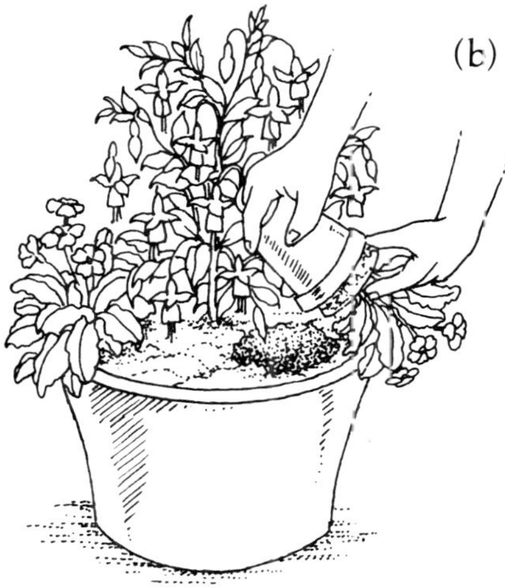

(b)

(c)

For a mixed planting, first place a drainage layer in the base of the container and fill with the correct soil to within 2cm (1in) of the rim. Plan the arrangement by placing the plants in their pots on top, taller ones in the centre, trailers at the edges. Dig holes with a trowel (a) to take the larger plants first, using their pots as a guide to size. Tap out each plant from its pot against the side of the container (b) and firm it into its prepared hole at the same depth as in the pot. Water-in the final arrangement (c) and cover the soil surface with peat or gravel to help retain moisture.

watered recently. The plant or plants it contains should be perky, upright, a good bright green, with leaves almost crisp to the touch and strong stems. If the plant is one that will flower, look for plenty of flower buds below the leaves. See that no roots are growing through the base of the container or sticking up in the air from the soil surface.

When you get your box or pot home, water it gently but

thoroughly, let it drain and then put it in a place out of wind and in slight shade until you are ready to put the plants into the containers you have chosen for them. If bad weather or pressure of time means that you have to delay your planting programme, examine your plants occasionally to make sure they have not attracted slugs or any of the insects which find them so appetizing.

Planting is a simple process which is almost exactly the same regardless of the size, shape or type of container. Always take the plants to the container, rather than the container to the plants. Make sure the container is filled with the correct soil and that this is well moistened. If necessary, water the plants once more – just a gentle sprinkle – before they are removed from their box or pot to be planted.

Bear in mind that filling a window box or other container with plants taken from a box or pot is a procedure comparable to your moving house; it involves a major upheaval for the plants and so everything possible should be done to minimize the considerable shock suffered by them. They should be treated gently and the tiny, hair-like roots which are their lifeline should be handled very carefully so that they suffer as little damage as possible.

Now, however, plants can sometimes be bought in small round or square containers made of a lightweight fibrous substance, rather than in plastic or terracotta pots. These pots are made of peat and they prevent any root damage because the plant is planted exactly as it is in its pot and the tiny root hairs grow easily and naturally through the pot into the soil that surrounds them. Other advantages are that the peat is impregnated with fertilizers and fungicides. There is more to be said about fibre pots in the section on raising your own plants.

When moving plants from the more usual plastic or terracotta pots it is essential to remove each plant with its ball of soil; the best way to do this is to hold the rim so that the plant's stem protrudes through your fingers and your palm is over the soil. Give the pot a sharp tap on some solid object while holding it upside down, and the plant with its neat root ball should fall into

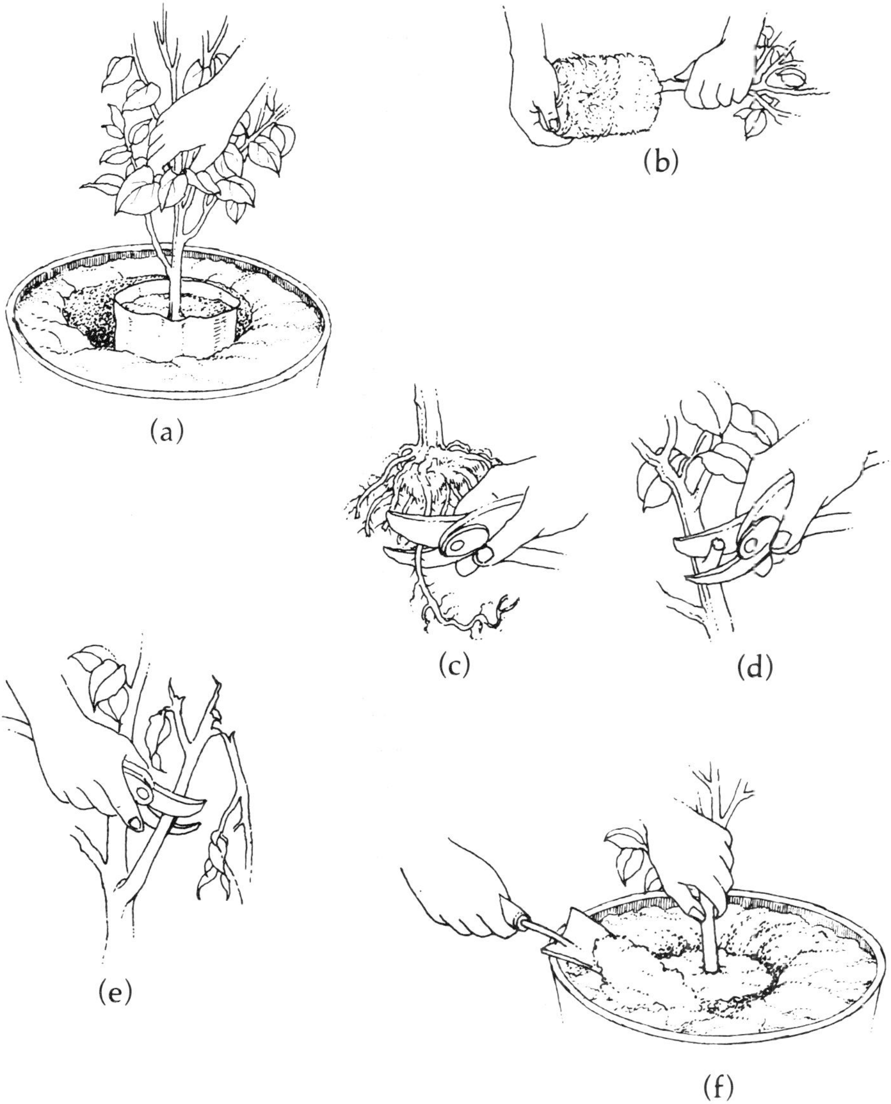

When planting shrubs or small trees (a) place the plant in its container in the prepared hole to ensure it is of adequate size. (b) Gently tease away excess soil from the roots. (c) Shorten any over-long roots. Cut away (d) any 'hat peg' snags and remove (e) any broken branches, cutting back to the main stem, as with (d). Firm the soil around the newly planted rocts (f) and then water the plant in.

your hand. This should then be placed gently into the hole you have previously prepared in the soil. Firm the soil around the plant at the same level as it was in the pot until the plant is upright and securely anchored. If plants in boxes are being moved, dig them out very gently using the point of a trowel or even a kitchen spoon, keeping as much soil as possible around the little roots. Hold the plant very gently by the leaves and place it in the prepared hole. When the container is fully planted, water it gently and, if possible, either keep it out of the sun or give it some light and dappled shade for the first day or two.

Once in position, the plants should not be moved until they have finished flowering or have died down in winter, unless they are perennials which may outgrow their containers. Ideally, you should plan all your containers in advance. You should see in your mind's eye the whole completed container, plant against plant, colour against colour, texture and height in blending unity.

For double the display of flowers, plant bulbs in two layers in a tub. Note the good drainage layer beneath, essential for bulbs which will rot in wet soil.

Colours and textures are largely a matter of personal taste, but there are a few sensible general rules about height which can best be illustrated by a somewhat extreme example. If a window box is thickly planted with pansies and extra height is required, you would not place a row of dwarf conifers along the front because they would hide the pansies and would look stern and rigid.

Instead, you would probably plant one or two of these at the back.

Remember that gardening on a small scale is a highly concentrated form of gardening. Every container must count and should make a constant display. Plants should be put out just before they reach their peak and be removed directly they have passed it, to allow space for other fresher plants.

As we have said, the time will come when some of your more permanent plants outgrow their containers. The roots may begin to appear through the drainage holes or above the soil surface. When this happens the plant can cease to grow, but it sometimes remains alive for a considerable period. Try to give it a new, larger home, another pot or tub with greater space for the roots. Remove the plant carefully, retaining a good root ball of soil and place it in a prepared planting hole in the new container, sifting fresh soil around the roots as you settle them in.

Make sure that the planting depth is the same as it was before and that the roots fit snugly into their new home with soil closely in contact with every part. Water-in gently.

If your plant is already growing in the largest container you can accommodate, try cutting back some of the roots and then replacing the plant in its original container. Simply remove the plant, prize the soil away from its roots with your fingers and then, using secateurs, cut back some of the longest, thickest roots so that the total area is reduced. You are unlikely to damage the plant by doing this because these roots mainly secure it in the soil and it is the finer, hair-like roots that carry out the essential task of nourishing the plant.

We have already mentioned the removal of plants which have passed their best and their replacement with plants just coming to their peak. It is always worth keeping a reserve of plants for this purpose, plants which have been bought, say, two or three weeks later than those already on display, so that they will be at their best when their predecessors are finishing. If you have room to grow from seed (see pp 87–9), then sow it at intervals so that the plants mature in succession. But if space is at such a premium that you cannot either keep a reserve of plants or grow from seed, you may be able to make arrangements with a local florist or nurseryman to produce plants to your requirements.

Once you have established a pleasing and satisfactory pattern for your containers, one which is worth following over the years, the ideal would be to maintain two identical containers, one for display and one kept in reserve, ready to replace the first when necessary. This might take some organizing, but it would ensure that the display as a whole would always be at its peak.

In some countries, it is quite impossible to grow a colourful display of flowers outside in winter, so when the frosts arrive it is best to remove your summer and autumn plants and replace them with those that will stand harsh weather. It is usually possible to underplant your winter evergreens with spring flowering bulbs, so that as the days begin to lengthen they can push their way up through the heathers or the ivies and provide an early taste of spring. A very rough guide for bulb planting depths is twice the diameter of the bulb, with one or two exceptions, such as the stem rooting types of lily, which should go a little deeper. All bulbs like good drainage, so when you have made your planting hole pour in a little bed of sharp sand and stand the bulb on this before covering it with soil.

Planting Strawberry and Potato Barrels

Somewhat different techniques from normal are required when planting strawberry and potato barrels. These are worth knowing about because it is always satisfying to grow your own fruit and vegetables, even in small quantities and, in addition, a well-planted strawberry barrel can look so attractive covered first with pretty white flowers and then with red fruit. Place one on a patio rather than a balcony or roof, because weight can be an important consideration. If possible, mount a strawberry barrel on a wheeled platform of some kind so that it can be turned regularly to allow sunlight to reach all of it.

A traditional strawberry pot is a pretty addition to a sunny patio. Protect the fruit from birds with nets and keep the soil moist by watering from the top and, if necessary, through each of the holes.

The traditional terracotta or earthenware strawberry pot is exactly the same as the more modern barrel, having a number of holes around its circumference in which the plants grow, but the pot is a little easier because each of the holes is provided with a slight lower lip to support the plants rather than simply a flat opening. However, both are planted in the same way, although subject to major differences in drainage and watering systems. The terracotta pot often has no drainage layer in the base, which means that a good layer of drainage material (broken crocks or pebbles) about 8cm (3in) deep must be placed in the base to provide a reservoir of moisture for the soil above. Begin to fill the pot with standard potting compost (see pp 23–4) until the first hole has been reached, insert the plant roots and firm the soil around them until the little strawberry plant is held secure and the foliage rests on the lip of the pot. Water each plant as your work proceeds; add more soil and go on to the next hole, treating it in exactly the same way, and so on up to the top of the pot or barrel.

After planting, it can be watered from the top, but if it is allowed to become too dry, it will be necessary to water it through each of the planting holes until all the soil is moist and it will again accept water from the top instead of shedding it from the dry surface. Better still, stand the pot in a dish and allow it to paddle from time to time. The planting and maintenance of parsley or herb pots is the same.

The modern type of strawberry barrel usually overcomes drainage problems by having a central core which is filled with

(a) (b)

Place a 15cm (6in) drainage layer and then another 15cm of peat-based compost in your potato barrel before planting 4 or 5 seed potatoes. Cover with moist compost and water lightly. Every time the shoots grow another 15cm (a) cover them with compost to the tips, until the top of the barrel is reached. Feel inside to test the potatoes for size when the plants have flowered (b).

drainage material. This core is the source of water for the remainder of the barrel, spreading out into the soil around it. When your strawberry plants begin to bear fruit, you can protect them from birds by using nets.

A potato barrel is a little different, for it has no holes around the sides. Some of the proprietary barrels do not have a base and are supposed to be stood directly on the bare soil. This is, of course, impossible on a balcony or a roof and frequently impossible even on a patio, so either choose a model with a base and drainage holes or fit your own. Small plastic laundry or rubbish bins, obtainable at department stores and hardware shops make excellent potato barrels, and are inexpensive and long lasting.

Insert the usual drainage layer to a depth of about 15cm (6in) and then your planting medium. This should be a fairly light mixture with additional peat and plenty of sand for good drainage, and it should be fairly rich, with at least one handful of a balanced fertilizer well mixed in with the compost. Ensure that there is about 15cm (6in) of soil above the drainage layer and on this soil place your seed potatoes, usually about four or five for the average sized barrel. Cover them with another 15cm (6in) of moist soil and water the surface lightly. The young potato shoots will appear above this surface and should be allowed to grow up to 15cm (6in) or so before more soil is added, just enough to leave the very tips of the growth showing. Do this each time until you reach the top of the barrel. When the plants have flowered you can begin to think about your crop.

Try them for size before digging them all up. Insert your arm deep into the compost and feel around, testing the size of the potatoes with your fingers. If you think them large enough, then harvest them all. Usually it is best to bring up just a few from this first testing, to enjoy them fresh, small, young and flavoursome. Leave the others in place to grow larger and only when you think they have reached their optimum size should you harvest them all.

Use the soil in the barrel as a part of a compost for some other container, together with fresh soil. Do not attempt to grow another potato crop in the same soil.

Watering and Feeding

Watering is undoubtedly the most difficult and pressing problem for the small scale gardener. Consider the difference between a plant growing in the soil of a garden and the same plant growing in a window box or other container. The first has unlimited space for its roots which can (and sometimes do) travel surprising distances and depths to seek the moisture they need. These roots have a constant source of natural foods from the soil. The plant is protected to a considerable extent from harsh winds and from too strong a sun by the plants around it, and it is watered and cleansed by the natural rains. But the plant in your container can stretch its roots only a short distance to look for the moisture it sometimes desperately needs. The soil in which these roots grow may be alternately bone dry and soaking wet and the artificial foods it holds are constantly washed from the soil and then, hopefully, replaced by the gardener, so drought and flood are sometimes accompanied by starvation and glut. Winds are more severe at window box and balcony level, yet protection is slight and the sun either burns down or is completely shaded away by the angles of the building.

Always water accurately, spraying the soil rather than the plants themselves. In strong sunlight, each drop acts as a magnifying glass and may cause burn marks on leaves and petals.

One method which helps to overcome this problem is to provide a surface mulch which will reduce moisture loss through evaporation and will also help to keep roots cool. This mulch can consist of moist peat or pulverized bark, but this would soon dry out and be blown away on a rooftop or balcony. It would therefore need to be held down and protected from sun and wind by a further mulch on top, this layer consisting of granite chips or graded pea gravel, as mentioned in our section on soils and composts, to a depth of at least 1cm (½in). The peat or bark would then be sure to absorb and hold moisture. Gravel or chippings can be obtained from most garden centres or from sand and gravel merchants. It looks pleasant and, with some care, can be saved from year to year and used again and again.

Always apply water to a container until it flows out from the drainage centre. As they dry out, most of the peat-based composts form a kind of crust or impervious layer around the root ball and a mere light watering sometimes cannot penetrate this to reach the dry roots within. If you notice that water rushes through the container at unusual speed, stop and prick the surface lightly with a trowel to allow water to penetrate, or come back after a few minutes and apply more water, by which time the crust should have softened enough to allow water through to the roots.

You can buy automatic drip watering equipment with one or more nozzles for each container. These will drip water at a pre-set rate and keep the soil always moist. This equipment is quite expensive, but the main objection to its installation is that it involves the snaking around, between and above your containers of a hose pipe, admittedly of a small calibre, but nevertheless an eyesore and a hindrance. It can be arranged in place for use during the night and removed in the morning, but its positioning and the setting of the drips takes time. In my opinion, this type of equipment is only really useful when you go away for a week or two. Without it, you would have to arrange for someone to come in and water your plants once or twice a day. It is possible to fix drip watering equipment so that it keeps all your containers moist during this time with very little chance of anything going wrong. Unfortunately, it seems to be impossible to hire this equipment for short periods.

If drip watering is used, make sure that no container is standing in a saucer or any other receptacle for collecting waste water, for this saucer would be kept continuously filled and before very long the plants in the container would begin to die. It has already been explained that the roots of all living plants require both moisture and air for their existence, and as waterlogged soil contains no air the plants drown. If any saucer, drip tray or similar contrivance has water in its base for more than an hour or so, empty it out and allow the plant to breathe again.

Another way in which water can be a problem is in the case of ericaceous plants — those that can only grow satisfactorily in an acid soil. Most tap water contains greater or lesser amounts of lime. This water can be perfectly all right for many plants, and indeed beneficial for some, but if used constantly on lime-haters it will eventually kill them.

It is always worthwhile then to collect as much clean rain-water as possible. Collect too much rather than too little, for after only a few days of hot, sunny weather a small supply will be exhausted and it will be necessary to resort to tap water again. But do not worry too much about this. Tap water will do little harm to ericaceous plants for a week or two in summer each year. It is the continuous use of water containing lime which they cannot tolerate.

The vital necessity of lavish watering creates another problem. This water washes through the soil and out of the drainage holes in the containers, taking with it plant foods from the soil which must be constantly replaced. This can prove expensive, so ways should be sought to minimize the cost.

The easiest way to feed all container grown plants is by means of a liquid fertilizer which is added to the water. The greater part of this liquid feed will pass straight through the soil and out with the water, leaving very little behind to nourish the plants, so if this water is collected, it can be used again. A simple way of doing this is to place smaller containers inside a large bucket when they are watered. Alternatively, you can apply fertilizer water more carefully and in lesser quantities than water alone. It should be noted that fertilizer must never be applied to any plant in a really dry soil, as it can damage the roots, so it is sensible to water all plants thoroughly first and then go round them once again with fertilizer-enriched water, giving them much less on this occasion.

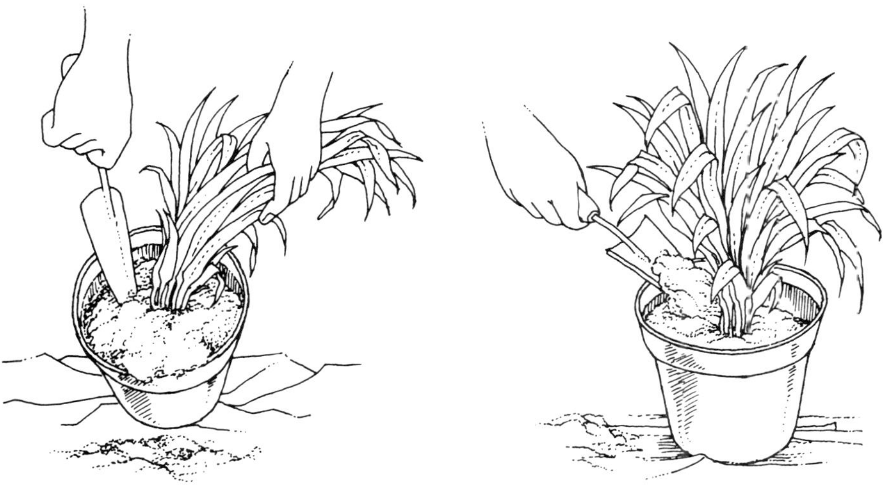

(a) (b)

After about two years, container soil can become exhausted and need freshening. Place a polythene sheet under the container and tilt it slightly. Using a trowel, scrape away up to 5cm (2in) of soil (a), being careful not to damage the plant's roots. (b) Replace with fresh soil.

Another answer is to use a granular form of fertilizer. This is easily obtainable and more or less comparable in price with liquids. Apply it in the recommended quantities to the soil surface. The instructions frequently advise that it should be gently raked into the soil, but there are two reasons why this advice should be disregarded. Firstly, you may have placed a moisture-saving mulch of pea gravel, or some such material, on the soil surface. This would have to be disturbed, or even removed, for the granules to be raked into the soil. And, secondly, the plants are going to be watered at least once a day under normal circumstances and this is going to carry the chemicals in the granules down into the soil just as efficiently as any raking.

Some fertilizers are available in the form of pills, pellets or sticks. One or more of these is pushed into the soil according to instructions and will break down very slowly under successive waterings, releasing small amounts of fertilizer into the soil. I have not myself found any of these to be very satisfactory, but I willingly admit that this may be a personal prejudice.

A further method of feeding plants is by means of what are known as foliar feeds – liquid sprays made up in solution and applied to the leaves of plants instead of to the soil. These are quick-acting and some have special purposes, such as giving the necessary iron to lime-hating plants or magnesium to aid fruit formation. Foliar feeds are not expensive but applying them can be a time-consuming business. Remember that they should not be used in bright sunlight as the sun's heat on the droplets may scorch the leaves.

Most fertilizers, however, contain suitable proportions of nitrogen, phosphates and potassium (usually known as N.P.K.) plus trace elements such as iron, magnesium, sulphur and manganese. You can buy fertilizers with a greater proportion of nitrogen for strong foliage growth, or a greater proportion of phosphates or potassium for better flowers, fruit and root growth. But, in general, a plant food with a 7:7:7 balance will suit all plants at all times.

As regards how often you should feed your plants, liquid fertilizers should be applied about once a week during the growing season from spring to late summer, and granular fertilizers roughly once a month during the same season; double the intervals during the rest of the year.

It is an interesting fact, though, that food is less important to plants than either water or light. Using too little fertilizer may result in a plant which is not at its best, but it will continue to live nonetheless. On the other hand, too much food can be as harmful as too much water, for it can burn the delicate root hairs or cause soft, sappy growth in a plant. Thin, elongated stems, pale foliage and an exhausted appearance can all be signs of over-feeding. It can also mean that leaves rather than flowers are produced.

General Maintenance

One of the major delights of small scale gardening compared to ground level gardening on a larger scale is that there are fewer plants, which means that you can get to know each one with some degree of intimacy. You can actually follow the development of a single plant over the days, as its leaves uncurl and the flower buds swell and burst into bloom. You can learn to understand the differing requirements of each plant, so that you expect this one to love the sun and that one to flourish in the shade. You will find that each has its own personality, which makes your gardening so much more pleasurable and interesting.

It is, of course, a good idea to establish some kind of a maintenance pattern or programme in your care of your roof garden or window box, your hanging baskets or your balcony patch. To water thoroughly and to feed are vital activities and when outside interests or duties intrude these may be your sole connection with gardening. But, if possible, try to go more deeply into things and you will be amply repaid.

If you have chosen the right containers, used the right soil mixtures, watered thoroughly and fed your plants into a state of sturdy good health, it should be a simple and quick matter to deal with them so that they maintain their state of health. But there are still a few little points which should be watched in the daily care programme of your small scale garden.

Do make it daily care if you can. A great deal can happen in 24 hours. Give each and every plant a close examination at least once a day. When you get to know your plants, something will tell you if things are going wrong: the colour of a leaf, the twist of a stem, the distortion of a new shoot, an unaccustomed mould on the soil surface. Immediate attention is almost certain to clear any trouble which could result in serious problems. Remember that greenfly can multiply at an astonishing rate and where a few can do little damage to a healthy plant, many could kill it.

Because plants are comparatively few in a small scale garden, it is essential that they perform well. One means of ensuring a constant succession of flowers is a rigorous dead-heading of all blooms that are drooping or dead. If they are left on the plant the flowers will develop into seed heads, and the energies of the plant will go into the production of seed rather than more flowers. Bear in mind that the function of every growing thing is the reproduction of its species. Colourful flowers are not there primarily for the delight of humans but to attract insects to fertilize them so that seed can be produced to ensure another generation of plants. Under normal circumstances, this seed is unnecessary because better quality seed can be obtained from a packet.

While dead-heading your plants you may notice a broken stem here or a wounded one there. You may see a new shoot bent double because it has been caught against a support, or one which is growing so much in the wrong direction that it is sure to interfere with the growth of nearby plants. Correct this by removing it completely; cut it at the point where it joins the parent stem, for if you merely trim it you may simply cause it to grow with increased vigour. Surgery at an early stage is easily shrugged off by the plant and greater trouble is avoided later. Every time you cut away any portion of plant material remove it completely and place it in your rubbish receptacle, preferably a light plastic bucket or a plastic sack. Do not let it remain on the surface of your container where it can pick up and spread disease.

One of the ways of helping taller plants to look neat and well cared for is to arrange supports for them as they grow. Without these, they can become wind-blown and broken and may damage neighbouring plants. Container grown plants seldom require stout, obvious stakes to hold them upright. A slim split cane will usually give adequate support or, at the most, a bamboo cane should be all that is necessary. These can be pushed into the soil and will stand rigidly enough to support a slim or whippy stem. Use soft green string as a tie for delicate plants and wire-centred twist stems for more woody ones; on the rare occasions when a tree or shrub has to be braced, use a purpose-made plastic tree tie obtainable from garden centres.

If the container is large enough to hold a generous display of blooms, it may be possible to use that well-known gardeners trick of inserting a few spreading twigs into the soil so that the foliage

(a) (b) (c) (d)

Encourage plants to grow attractively by giving them some support. Twigs pushed into the soil (a) help flowers stand upright and are soon hidden by new growth. (b) Train runner beans up strings attached to the sides of the tub and tied to the top of a central pole. (c) Use soft twine to tie a soft-stemmed plant, such as a pelargonium, to a cane at 15cm (6in) intervals. (d) Climbers such as clematis can be fastened to strong horizontal wires with paper-covered ties or plastic rings.

and flowers grow through them gaining hidden support but still looking absolutely natural.

Special galvanized wire supports can be bought from garden centres and seed stores. These stand on three legs and have a flat grid at the top with plenty of space through which stems, foliage and flowers can grow, thus completely hiding the metal while being held up by it. It is not necessary for these supports to be pushed into the soil. Several variations on this theme are available.

'Pinching out' is an alternative way of controlling tall plants. It is a form of pruning which involves removing the tip of the leading

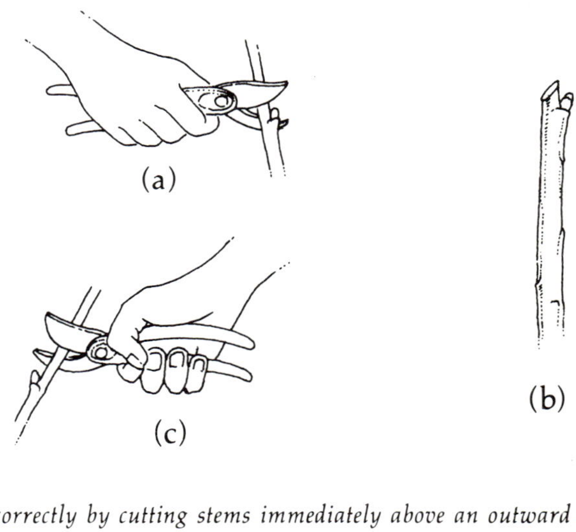

Prune correctly by cutting stems immediately above an outward pointing bud (a) to achieve this result (b). Cut incorrectly like this (c), and a length of stem remains which will die back and can damage the main stem.

shoot or the terminal bud, the purpose being to encourage more and stronger shoots to grow lower down the plant or to stimulate the production of larger blooms. When carried out early in the season, it will produce a bushy, leafy plant rather than a tall and spindly one. If done later in the season, it tends to result in larger, more plentiful flowers and better berries or fruits.

Most of the plants grown on a balcony or patio will be herbaceous or bulbous and will not require the more formal pruning demanded by some trees and shrubs if they are to look their best and be productive. But even the roof or patio gardener may wish to have, say, a clipped conifer or a shaped bay tree in a tub, and the balcony gardener may grow a favourite rose in a large pot, so it is worth understanding the basic principles of pruning. Severe pruning results in strong and vigorous growth; gentle pruning will generate less growth but a greater quantity of flowers or fruit. So the small scale gardener will normally be advised to prune lightly to get the best results from permanent plants grown in containers.

Some flowering shrubs should be cut back immediately after they have flowered, whether in spring or autumn. This will encourage the growth of new, strong shoots for next year's blooms and, at the same time, will clear away the dead or dying flowers and shoots to avoid any risk of disease. Low growing shrubs, such as heathers and lavenders, need a light trimming after flowering to neaten their appearance and encourage better flowers next season.

Climbers such as ivy need no more than a light trimming to shape. Summer flowering species such as jasmine and honeysuckle need no real pruning other than the removal of old, wounded, dead or diseased shoots. Growth may be tied in at the same time. Clematis pruning depends entirely on the type. Check on this before going to work with the secateurs, or you may lose a season's flowers.

If you grow a rose in a pot or tub, keep it well dead-headed and while doing this cut back the stem by no more than about one third to encourage new growth. Prevent wind damage in winter by cutting all stems back when the frosts begin to about half their height, as well as cutting away all old, diseased, weak or rubbing branches. Again, remember to clear away all prunings, especially fallen leaves, which can harbour the pests and diseases which will damage your plants in the next season.

Controlling Pests and Diseases

On the basis that prevention is better than cure, the best way of ensuring clean, healthy plants is to grow them well, so that they are sturdy, strong and capable of shrugging off any insect or disease attack that might come their way. Ensure adequate watering, feeding and light, cut away dead and dying flowers and stems, keep plants clean and you will find that they grow so strongly that even if attacked by greenfly, for example, they can sustain themselves until the pest is identified and cleared.

It is therefore far better to grow healthy plants right from the beginning than have to rely on chemical sprays or surgical treatments later on, so if among your healthy plants you notice one that appears to be in trouble, remove it at once and isolate it until you have been able to identify the problem. Then examine its neighbours carefully, paying particular attention to the undersides of their leaves.

Young, tender, succulent plants are more likely to attract pests than older, tougher specimens. The growing shoots are usually the danger points in younger plants. If you watch your plants closely at all times you will be able to spot an infestation of, say, aphids, before it has reached dangerous proportions and will be able to take immediate action before any vital damage has been done.

There are really very few pests and even fewer diseases that are likely to cause serious trouble to a moderately careful rooftop or balcony gardener, so there is no need to lay in a whole armoury of sprays and potions to combat them. It is surprising what good can be done with a simple spray of soap or detergent in water.

Buy garden chemicals, therefore, only in small quantities and always throw away old bottles or packs which have lost their labels. Always remember that insecticides are necessarily poisons. Some are highly dangerous if handled or used other than according to directions. Treat them with great respect. Never use an insecticide unless you know exactly what you are doing; never use any spray in a wind, even if it is only a light breeze, as it can easily be blown in your face or over other people; never leave any bottle or pack where it can be reached

Aphids and other pests often congregate on the underside of foliage, so when spraying make sure that the whole leaf is drenched. Hold back stems to reach the underside if necessary. Gardening gloves will protect your skin from chemicals and scratches from thorny plants. Wash out the sprayer thoroughly afterwards.

by children. Always wash your hands carefully after using an insecticide. The danger is not so much of any vital or long-term effect, but of minor skin, stomach or eye irritations, though wearing gardening gloves can reduce any risks to the skin of the hands. Whenever possible, apply insecticides only when there are no bees about, as these are very beneficial to plants, and this generally means spraying in the evenings shortly before dusk. Remember to wash out the sprayer thoroughly afterwards, using hot water and a detergent. Rinse it out very thoroughly as well.

Pests can be very roughly divided into four basic types, and diseases into three. Pests can be those that chew or bite plants, those that suck their sap, those that attack stems, flowers and fruit and those that attack roots. Diseases are bacterial, fungal or viral.

The main chewing pests are caterpillars; these are the larvae of various moths and butterflies. Some can do enormous damage and strip an entire tree of its foliage in a matter almost of hours. Most can be found and identified quickly when you notice that holes are beginning to appear in leaves. Although many are difficult to find at first because they blend so beautifully with the foliage on which they are feeding, once the eye has become educated it is possible to pick off the caterpillars by hand and dispose of them. If this is distasteful to you, or if you prefer to make quite sure that you have dealt with every caterpillar, do one of the following: dust with derris powder, spray with liquid malathion or with one of the easily obtainable proprietary insecticides.

Another chewing insect, which fortunately is not seen too frequently on patio or balcony, is the red spider mite. This is neither red nor a spider, but a tiny yellowish insect which can sometimes take on a reddish hue and may spin a fine web on the undersides of leaves where it is operating. Its effect is to distort and discolour leaves, making them dry and brittle. Normally, spider mites are found only where conditions are dry and warm, so they seldom appear where watering is the constant preoccupation of the gardener, but they sometimes seem not to know this. Malathion will clear them up.

Pests which suck the sap of your plants are mainly the aphids: greenfly and blackfly, which can multiply at such a rate that one or two seen in the morning can become a thousand by the evening, so it is wise to attack them directly they are seen. There are many types of aphids and they have many natural enemies: certain birds, and insects such as ladybirds. They congregate mainly on the tender, growing shoots of some (but not all) plants — greenfly on roses, for example, and blackfly on nasturtiums. They stick their long, needle-like noses into the surface of a leaf or stem and draw out the sap and, in so doing, they distort and discolour the growing tip. Even worse, they often spread virus diseases.

The best opponents of the aphids, apart from their natural enemies which should of course be encouraged, are the systemic insecticides. These, of which there are many, have a dual means of attack, for they both kill by contact and by being absorbed into the sap of the plant where they exist for up to four weeks or so, during which time any insect sucking this sap will be killed by the poison it contains.

Other members of this sucking group are woolly aphids and mealy bugs, both of which hide in the centre of a little woolly patch, white and easily identified. Whitefly, as the name suggests, are little white flies that rise in tiny clouds when disturbed. There are other sap suckers but the above are the most likely to be seen by the small scale gardener. All can be cleared by using a systemic insecticide, or one such as liquid malathion or derris dust. Equally, a minor infestation can be literally washed away by a dousing or spraying with plain water, a primary attack that is well worth trying.

Earwigs, thrips and chafers are the main insects that attack and eat holes in stems, flowers and fruit. Once again, systemic insecticides, malathion and derris are all suitable weapons.

The stem and root chewers are mainly slugs and snails. They can do enormous harm, wiping out a whole new planting in a single night. Because they work mainly at night and because they are masters at hiding themselves away, mainly below ground or in piles of dead leaves or other garden rubbish (if the small scale garden is not kept scrupulously clean), they are difficult to see and one must identify them by the damage they do. It is sometimes difficult to understand where they can come from, to appear in such numbers on a balcony, for instance, high above ground level. If in any doubt about them, scatter a few slug pellets about, or if you fear for birds or domestic pets, hide these under a stone or keep them otherwise away from pets but available to slugs and snails.

Plant diseases which might be encountered on a roof garden or balcony are few in number. They are almost entirely fungus, bacteria or virus originated. Among the fungi are mildews, scab, certain wilts, stem and root rots, peach leaf curl and rose black spot. None are really to be feared in small scale gardening, appearing largely in greenhouse gardening or among fruit trees. Proprietary fungicides are many and easy to apply. Some are used preventatively — for instance, against black spot on roses, before any evidence of the disease is seen, but this should not generally be necessary under conditions such as we are considering.

Bacterial and viral diseases are again little to be feared by the clean small scale gardener, which is just as well, for in general terms there is little one can do if disease from either of these sources is diagnosed. The best thing to do if you are certain that a bacterium or a virus has attacked any of your plants is to dig it up immediately and burn it, thus minimizing the possibility of what could be a disastrous spread of the disease.

Birds, cats, dogs and, let's face it, children can all be pests if we allow them to be. The methods which can be used to protect plants from their random activities are many and varied, but are basically a matter for each gardener to decide.

Raising Your Own Plants

When the idea of making a garden on a patio, balcony or roof first enters our heads the first thing we wish to do is rush out and buy some plants and containers so that we can get started. Indeed, this is probably the only way to begin. But after a time things calm down, we are in less of a hurry. The sheer expense of constantly buying new plants perhaps makes us begin to wonder whether it might be possible to raise certain plants ourselves from seed and to propagate others from cuttings which we can take from our own plants or beg from friends and neighbours.

Without a garden, without a greenhouse, with little spare space on a balcony or patio and less in the home, is it possible to raise one's own plants? The answer is yes, it is not only possible, it is easy so long as our ambitions are confined to the raising or propagation of certain types of plants and in limited quantities.

Seed sowing is undoubtedly the easiest and cheapest way of raising a number of plants for your window boxes or other containers. You will probably find that you produce far more plants than you actually need, but there will always be someone to whom you can give your surplus. The process takes a little time and a little space, so choose carefully what plants you wish to raise from seed; these should be ones that you will need in number rather than singly: petunias, cinerarias, impatiens, begonias, lobelia, yes, and tomatoes, cucumbers and marrows.

You will need a space indoors where the light is as good as possible but out of direct sun unless filtered through, say, a lace curtain. You will need some seed trays, some seed compost and some translucent plastic bags large enough to take the seed trays comfortably. You will also need the seeds, easy enough to obtain, and a number of little pots. The little black plastic 'sleeve' pots are excellent for this purpose. They occupy almost no space when empty, they are cheap, and even when they contain tiny plants they can still be squeezed into some convenient space without the plants coming to any harm. They can also be used again and again if you are prepared to clean and store them. More expensive, more space demanding, yet a considerable advantage in some ways are the little peat or fibre pots mentioned earlier (see p 64), which when planted with their growing seedling will become integrated with the soil and so cause no disturbance to the developing plant.

To plant your seeds, fill a seed tray with suitable compost (see pp 23–4), leaving just a little space at the top for watering. A layer of drainage material in the base is not necessary as the compost will be kept no more than just moist. Sprinkle the seeds on top of this as lightly as you can and cover them with only the finest layer of compost or sand. Finally, water the tray, but do this with a sprayer rather than a can, just a light misting so that the seeds and the soil around them are damp. Place this prepared seed tray inside a plastic bag, blow into it to keep the plastic away from the surface and then seal it with a rubber band. Always label the tray carefully, preferably inside the plastic bag rather than out, giving the name of the plant and the date on which the seed was sown.

At this stage it does not matter whether the as yet ungerminated seeds are in the light or not, so whether you place the plastic bag with its contents in an airing cupboard, on a window sill or in the bathroom makes no difference, so long as the situation is comparatively warm, preferably between 15° and 20°C (60-70°F) and free from draughts. It will not be necessary to water the plants while inside the plastic bag as this should maintain the humidity. If conditions inside the bag become too wet, take out the seed tray, turn the bag inside out, replace the tray and seal the bag again. When the seeds begin to grow, move the tray into a light spot if it has been in the dark.

Once the seedlings begin to look like real plants instead of a fuzz on the compost surface, open the bag a little during daylight hours. Place a pencil or a drinking straw inside to keep the plastic roof off the little plants. Gradually open the bag more and more or roll it back until you can finally remove the box and let the plants breathe the same air as you and I. Keep conditions just moist by watering as necessary with a sprayer.

When they are large enough to handle they can be moved on to individual pots, the little plastic sleeve pots just mentioned or the fibre pots. Plant one in each compost-filled pot and keep these together in another tray. When they begin to outgrow these pots, the plants can be moved on to their final homes in window boxes or other containers when the weather allows.

Some seeds – for plants such as nasturtiums and the pretty burning bush shrub – can be sown directly into outdoor containers and left to grow there, though it will obviously take some time before they reach display size. Some food crops,

(a)

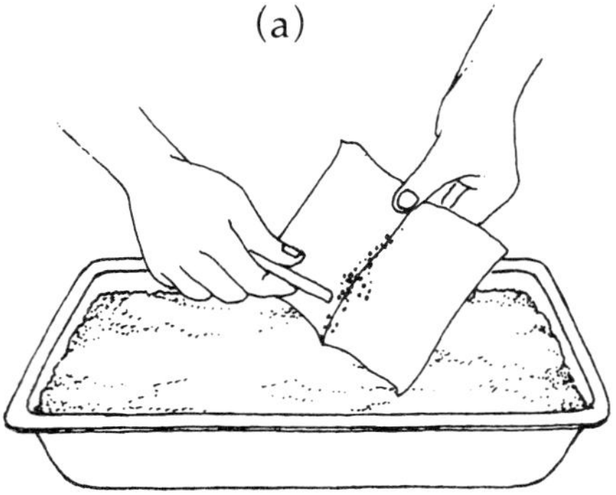

Grow from seed for economy and pleasure. (a) Scatter seeds thinly on the seed compost and cover lightly with compost or sand. Water gently with a sprayer.

(b) Place the seed tray in a plastic bag with a label giving the plant's name and date of sowing. Blow into the bag to raise it from the compost and seal with a rubber band. Place in daylight when the seeds germinate and open the bag a little.

(b)

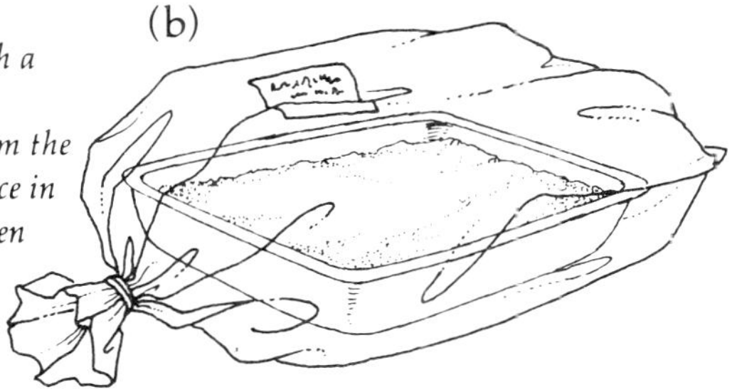

(c)

When the seedlings are large enough to handle (c), ease them out using a pencil, holding by the leaves, not the stem, and plant in individual 'sleeve' pots (d) prior to planting out in your containers.

(d)

particularly radishes, can also be sown directly into containers and growbags outdoors, saving space in your seed trays and pots.

The process of taking cuttings is in some ways even simpler than sowing seed and it means that a growing plant is produced instead of simply a seedling. But each cutting makes only one plant, whereas a sowing of seed can make many.

To take a tip or stem cutting choose a healthy and strongly growing shoot and cut away a piece up to 10cm (4in) long. Remove any lower leaves close to the main stem but do not touch any buds or bud cells. Have ready a small pot filled with your rooting medium, which can be cuttings compost, peat, sand, vermiculite, perlite or a mixture of some of these substances. Or you can use a comparatively new device known as a cuttings bag; similar to a miniature growbag, it consists of a small plastic sack filled with special cuttings compost, into which you insert the newly taken cutting through little slits made in the sides of the plastic. These cuttings bags are excellent and practically foolproof, but naturally enough they cost a little more than the materials for the basic process outlined above.

Going back to our pot filled with the rooting medium, make a small hole in this compost with a pencil, or something similar, and slip the base of the cutting into this hole, firming the soil around it carefully. Water it in and allow it to drain, then slip the pot into a transparent plastic bag and keep it in a warm and light place until new growth is seen. Where the plant to be propagated is somewhat woody it is helpful to use a hormone rooting powder. Merely dip the end of the cutting stem into this powder so that a little sticks to it and then drop it into the prepared hole as before. The rooting powder assists the rapid production of roots. You can tell when roots have started to grow both by the appearance of a new green at the growing tip of the plant and by giving it a very gentle pull. If there is slight resistance it means that new roots are anchoring it in place.

Many cuttings will root in water alone. Take a cutting as before and slip the base into a phial containing about 5-8cm (2-3in) of water and leave it there until you see that roots have been

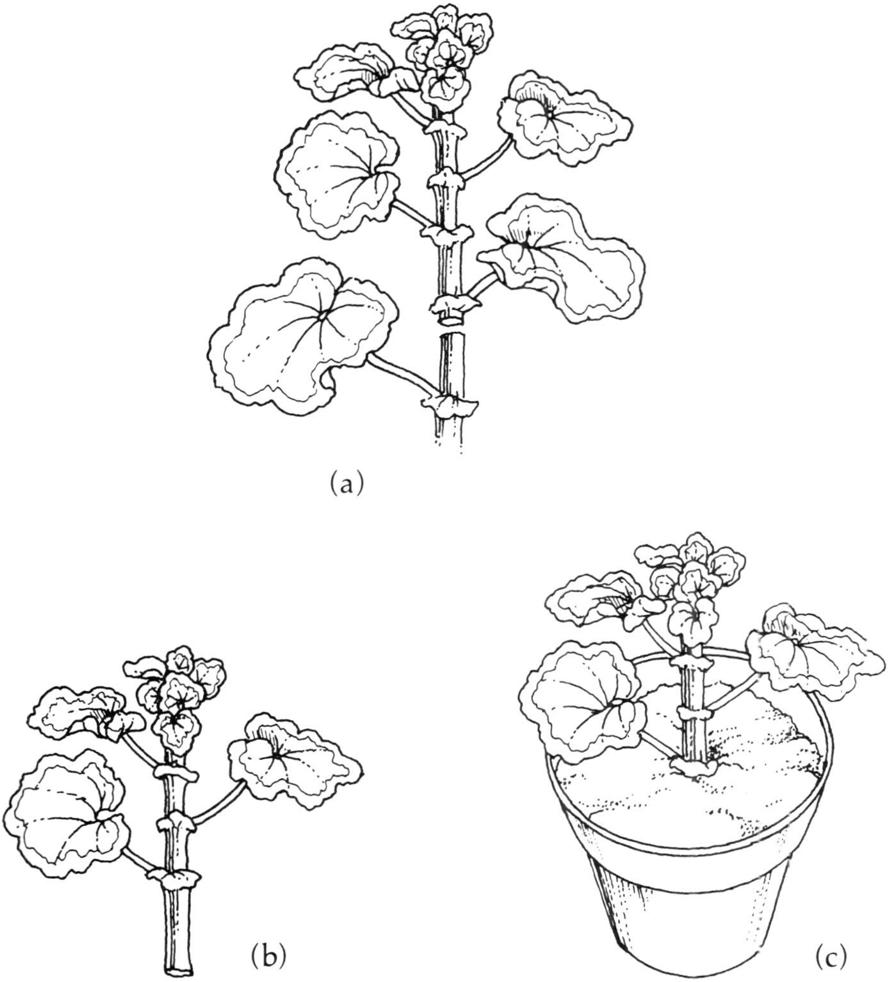

Pelargoniums (geraniums) can be raised both from seed and from cuttings. To take a cutting, (a) remove the top 15cm (6in) of a strong shoot just below a node or leaf joint. Strip off the lowest leaf or leaves (b) and bury the cutting almost up to the lowest remaining leaf in a suitable cuttings compost (c).

produced. The little plant can then be potted up in compost prior to planting out.

Another method of increasing your stock is called layering and it is really much the same as taking a stem cutting, except that the stem or shoot is not cut from the parent plant until it has produced its own roots. The technique here is to take a low growing stem of a plant, such as a rhododendron, and bend it down to the soil either on the ground or in a pot or tray. Make a slight split in the stem at some convenient point where it touches the soil and bury this, leaving the shoot in the air above the surface. If necessary, place a stone over the buried portion or fix it in place with a 'hairpin' made from a twig. At the point where you made the little split, new roots will grow into the soil, and when new growth shows that they are developing well, cut the portion leading to the parent plant. You will then be left with an entire new plant.

A few plants, such as strawberries, produce little runners at the ends of which baby plants grow. These too can be placed on, or pinned to, the soil and they will grow roots and develop into new plants which can be separated from the parent plant to grow successfully on their own.

Certain plants, particularly perennials — dwarf Michaelmas daisies and heleniums, for example — make a mass of roots after they have been growing for some time. If these grow too large for their container, the plants may start to die, choked by the pressure of their own roots. To avoid this, these roots can be divided into several sections, each of which can be potted up and will grow into smaller and quite separate plants which will flourish on their own.

Some plants are so eager to reproduce themselves that the species has several means to this end. Many bulbs produce smaller bulb replicas when they have been growing for some time and these little offspring can be separated to make another flowering plant in a year or two; clumps of bulbs around the original bulb can be divided and replanted, but some lilies produce bulbils on their stems which can be removed and planted. Climbers and trailers, such as ivies, will produce roots at many places along their stems, and if these roots touch the soil of a pot or window box they will begin to grow into it, making a new plant which can be cut away from the parent – self-layering, as it were.

Small Scale Gardening
PART V

PLANTS FOR THE SMALL SCALE GARDEN

♦

There are so many plants available for the small scale garden that this section can only cover a relatively small number of them. I have, however, aimed to include selections of the most popular and practical plants of various types – perennials, which continue from year to year; biennials, which are planted one year to flower and finish the next; and annuals which flower for one season only. The following must therefore be regarded as a varied foretaste of the wonderful variety of plants to be enjoyed in your small scale garden. In the larger garden centres, specialist advice can often be obtained and suitable plants will be grouped together on display so that you can see, for instance, just how many varieties of ivies or pelargoniums there are to choose from. The plants which you grow in your small scale garden are as much an expression of your personality as the way you decorate your home – and discovering the plants which suit you, and then seeing them grow, is always a delightful and rewarding experience.

Colourful Bulbs

Even a small selection of bulbs (the term also covers corms and tubers) will provide a display of surprisingly long-lasting flowers spread over many weeks. Some, like aconites, crocuses and dwarf irises, flower in the very early part of the year, brightening the short, dark days, and thus paying a handsome dividend for a small investment. Bulbs are mainly perennial, but they differ considerably in appearance, habit and season of growth. They come in sufficient variety to be suitable for every type of container. Many are very sweetly scented, though some are more flamboyant than others. So long as it is mature, every bulb is a potential flower and it should bloom within six months, possibly even less time than this, according to its type.

Most share an agreeable quality which is that although they can look decorative when grown on their own, they will grow with and among, even up through, other kinds of plants. This means that containers holding bulbs can also be well filled with other plants which remain leafy and decorative during the winter months while the bulbs are still underground. These companion plants can be evergreen, perhaps little conifers, small aucubas or euonymus, or hebes and heathers, the latter of which will also bloom in their season. Often more temporary but showy biennials are grown with the bulbs later to produce a harmonious colour scheme. These plants include forget-me-nots, wallflowers, double daisies and pansies. If they are planted deeply enough to begin with, some kinds of bulbs can be left undisturbed for years while seasonal planting goes on above them.

Snowdrops, crocuses and narcissi are quite good tempered when planted upon, as it were. When the time comes, summer bedding plants can be sown or planted among their fading leaves. When these leaves are brown and come away easily without tugging, they can be cleared and there will be no further sign of the bulbs until they begin to shoot in the following spring.

If, however, bulbs are grown in a small container, such as a window box, you may need to remove and store them for planting the next autumn to flower in spring; for information on storing, see p 47.

The earliest flowering kinds are all fairly short-stemmed and so come to little harm during winter and spring gales. However, unless a site is very well protected it is advisable to select only the shorter-stemmed varieties of such large-flowered kinds as tulips and daffodils. Hyacinths, being compact, are fairly secure, but even these, especially if the flower spikes are very dense and heavy, should sometimes be staked for safety. Avoid planting the very large-flowered varieties of tulips, since these behave like banners in a breeze and become badly torn.

Few scents are as romantic as those of lilies, even one or two plants of the right kind are enough to fill the air with a sweet and lingering perfume. Like so many other bulb flowers, they are delightfully varied, the species and varieties differing from each other in shape, size, colour and perfume. Many of the modern hybrids are gorgeously coloured. They make good container plants if the rules are followed.

Lily bulbs root in two ways. Some kinds produce roots only from the base of the bulb, but others produce roots from the base of the stems as they grow from the bulbs. Generally speaking, the latter are the best kind for container gardening.

Suitable lilies include the Asiatic hybrids, *auratum, auratum platyphyllum, bulbiferum croceum, formosanum pricei, hansonii,* Honeydew, Jamboree strain, *longiflorum* varieties, *martagon album, nepalense,* Potomac hybrids, *regale, pumilum, speciosum* hybrids (greatly recommended), *testaceum* and Verona. All of these grow best in peat-based compost.

Use roomy containers. Take flower pot sizes as a guide. For instance, a 15cm (6in) pot is suitable for a single bulb. A 20-25cm (8-10in) pot is needed for three bulbs or more. Lilies can be potted from early autumn until mid-spring.

When planting the stem rooting kinds it is best not to completely fill the container. Instead, allow space so that the soil may be top dressed as the roots appear on the stem above the original soil level. This way they can be kept safely covered.

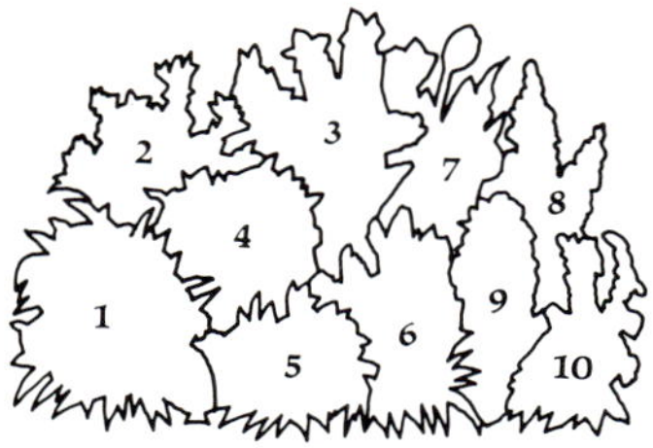

1. Snowdrop (*Galanthus nivalis*). Perennial. Height: 15cm (6in). Flowers early to mid-spring in sun or shade. Plant bulbs in autumn.

2. Glory of the snow (*Chionodoxa luciliae*). Perennial. Height: 15cm (6in). Flowers early to mid-spring in sun. Plant bulbs in autumn.

3. Daffodils (*Narcissi*), in great variety, including miniatures. Height 8–60cm (3in–2ft). Flowers early spring to early summer in sun or partial shade. Plant bulbs from early summer to mid-autumn.

4. Iris (*Iris reticulata*). Perennial. Height: 23cm (9in). Flowers mid-spring in sun. Plant bulbs in autumn.

5. Crocus, in great variety. Perennial. Height: 15cm (6in). Flowers early to mid-spring in sun. Plant bulbs in autumn.

6. Graph hyacinth (*Muscari botryoides*). Perennial. Height: 15–20cm (6–8in). Flowers in early spring in sun. Plant bulbs in early autumn.

7. Tulips (*Tulipa*), in great variety. Perennial. Height: 15–45cm (6in–1ft 5in). Flowers late spring to early summer in sun. Plant bulbs in early autumn.

8. Wallflowers (*Cheiranthus cheiri*). Biennial. Height: 30–60cm (1–2ft). Flowers in spring sun. Sow seed indoors in mid-spring.

9. Hyacinth (*Hyacinthus orientalis*) and varieties. Perennial. Height: 15–20cm (6–8in). Flowers early to mid-spring in sun. Plant bulbs in autumn.

10. Forget-me-nots (*Myosotis alpestris* and others). Perennial treated as a biennial. Height: 15–30cm (6in–1ft). Flowers from spring to summer in partial shade. Sow seed outdoors in early summer to flower in the following year.

Begin by filling the container a quarter full with drainage material, then half fill it with the potting medium. Place the bulbs on this, keeping them at least 5cm (2in) apart. Cover them with no more than about 1cm (½in) of soil at first planting. From then on just add more soil as is necessary. Keep the soil just moist until you see the shoots, then water the plants moderately until they are in full growth. After this, they should be freely watered until they have flowered when the quantity should be reduced again. Keep the plants almost dry and away from frosts from late autumn to early spring, then each year in either autumn or spring turn out the bulbs from the pots and repeat the process using fresh soil. An exception is the stately *L. longiflorum*, which should not be kept dry. Repot this species and any of its varieties annually in early autumn.

Should you wish to grow other plants at a later date with lilies, you should be careful not to disturb or harm the bulb roots in any way. The following method prevents undue damage and it can

All the freshness of spring is in this glowing floral mixture, mainly of early flowering bulbs, which include snowdrops, crocuses, hyacinths, grape hyacinths, daffodils, and Glory of the snow, together with popular bedding plants such as colourful, sweetly scented wallflowers and dainty forget-me-nots.

also be used for any other bulbs, or even plants of a more permanent nature, such as shrubs, to which you may like to add floral interest. Fill the container to the required depth for the first planting of bulbs, or to accommodate the root ball of a plant. Set the bulbs or plant on the surface of the soil. Then, to mark the sites of bedding plants and others which may be planted at some future date, arrange empty flower pots with their rims level with the rim of the container. So that the soil over the bulbs or around the plant does not dry out too quickly, part fill the flower pots with soil. At planting time, simply lift out the flower pots and fill each space with a little potting compost and a new plant.

Bulb flowers are not limited to spring and early summer. There are others that bloom in summer and early autumn. Some of these are delightfully scented. These include the 1m (3ft) high summer hyacinth or *Galtonia candicans* which flowers from midsummer to early autumn; the white, wine-purple-centred acidanthera flowering a little later and the multi-coloured freesias, both double and single flowered. For colour and fascination there are also the showy poppy anemones, dahlias, the pineapple flower or eucomis, stately gladioli, several irises, ixias, lilies already mentioned, nerines, amaryllys or belladonna lily and, finally, possibly the most extravagent looking flowers of all, the great rose-like double begonias. Tubers of the last can be started indoors, potted on and planted outside when all fears of frosts are past. The other kinds can be planted directly into their containers and left to grow outdoors.

Generally speaking, bulbs are not suitable for hanging baskets, mainly because so many of them grow upright and look unattractive displayed at an angle. However, there are some which give quite spectacular results. Tulips, for instance, whose stems are so apt to curve when the flowers are cut and arranged in water, will also curve when planted in a hanging basket, those at the base turning their flowers upwards to the light. The short stemmed kinds, particularly the early double varieties and the showy early species, are best. Forget-me-nots can be grown with them and these will also curve around. The large and showy Dutch crocuses may also be grown this way, although these are usually displayed in terracotta crocus or strawberry pots. The final effect is much the same, the plants in the holes at the lowest levels curving upwards prettily and masking the surface of the container.

The basket should be planted all over the surface as well as in the top, with the tips of all the bulbs pointed outwards. Begin at the base, add lining moss and a little soil, place one bulb pointing downwards at the very centre about 2.5cm (1in) from the surface, then continue lining the basket, adding the soil and the bulbs, securing each in position by covering it with soil before the others are arranged in place. When you reach 5-8cm (2-3in) from the rim of the basket, plant a few more to grow up in the normal way.

Bedding Plants

The most popular bedding plants for small scale gardening fall into the half-hardy annuals group and must be protected from the frost. The reason why these are more widely grown than the frost-resistant hardy annuals is that they have a much longer flowering period, most of them lingering on until the frosts, while the hardy kinds will have already seeded and faded. They have to be sown early in the year and under sheltered conditions. Some need a higher germination temperature than others. Commercially, these are all greenhouse grown. However, it is possible to raise most of them on a sunny window sill in a warm room. If they need high temperatures, the seed trays and, later, the little potted seedlings can be kept inside inflated, closed plastic bags which act as micro-greenhouses and provide both warmth and humidity. My own fibrous rooted begonias, petunias, impatiens, salpiglossis and many others are raised this way.

The only problem is that of space. One is apt to find that every window sill in the house has become a little nursery for some weeks. So both the gardener and the plants benefit if an early start is made in hardening them off so that they become acclimatized to outdoor life. As soon as they are large and sturdy enough, stand them out in the sunshine, well protected from any draughts, and bring them indoors in the evenings before the temperature drops. Do not stand them outside if the temperature is low and when you bring them in, make sure they are stood in a place where they will receive daylight in the mornings.

As with flowers grown from bulbs, it is wise in most cases to select those kinds which will not grow too tall. Plants which have to be heavily staked and tied are most unsightly in a container. Bear in mind that one can add to the area of colour in any container by setting trailing and scrambling plants near the rims so that both foliage and flowers cascade down over the exterior. Trailing lobelias are a favourite for this role — and there are many varieties in a mixture of colours, as well as popular Cambridge and sapphire blue and a purple-red with a white eye. But there are others which also provide contrasts of form and colour; these include amaranthus or love-lies-bleeding, pendulous begonias, *Phlox drummondii*, gazania, verbena and the shrubby marguerite, *Chrysanthemum frutescens*.

Sometimes plants which grow fairly upright or wide spreading at the centre of a container will obligingly spill over it if planted at the edge. Impatiens, vivid and long lasting, mesembryanthemum (Livingstone daisies), nemophila, pansies, petunias (infinite variety, wonderful colours, sweet scents), phacelia and tropaeoleum or nasturtium, even sweet peas, are examples. Misty blue ageratum is a good mixer to plant with any of these. Another great favourite which also offers several colours and variation of foliage is the ivy leaved pelargonium or geranium.

Flamboyant, varied and delicately perfumed, petunias are extremely popular summer bedding plants, seen growing here in large hand-painted cans. They like plenty of sunshine and their soil should be kept moist.

These zonal pelargoniums (geraniums), with attractive bands of colour on their foliage, are combined with the trailing, ivy-leaved type in an eye-catching container. The many varieties of pelargonium can be raised either from seed or from cuttings.

The handsome and showy pelargoniums or pot geraniums are always to be seen on sale. It is possible also to raise these from seed at home. They need an even temperature of about 21-24°C (70-75°F) to germinate quickly and evenly. They will flower in early summer if sown at the start of spring. Colours range from pure white through pretty apple blossom pinks, salmon, cerise, scarlet and purple-red and most recent of all, yellow. Pelargoniums are killed by frost and so have to be renewed each year, though they can be raised from cuttings taken from the previous year's plants, as shown on page 91.

They are divided into several groups which are quite easy to recognize. Those with leaves which are marked with a dark or contrasting zone of colour, sometimes just a faint band of darker green, are called zonal pelargoniums. Those which are often seen in hanging baskets or scrambling over a container, or in warm districts even climbing up a trellis, are ivy leaved pelargoniums. These are varied in their turn, some having pretty foliage.

The tricolour varieties have three distinct hues in their leaves. These are very lovely although they do not usually have such fine blooms as the zonals. Bicolours have green and white leaves.

New varieties are constantly being introduced and we can expect to find some which will not fit into the groups described above. For instance, some now have double flowers.

Annuals for Fragrance

Most of the very showy annuals, or plants treated as annuals, are scentless or almost so. However, stocks, nicotiana, antirrhinums and most petunias have a delightful fragrance and few annuals are as sweetly scented as some of the little ground-hugging alyssum varieties, the familiar white flowered, the purple Oriental Night, Rosie O'Day, a pretty deep pink, in particular. All the tagetes, including the French and African marigolds, and pot marigolds, have a pungent scent, more detected when the foliage is bruised than from the blooms themselves. Unlike many other climbing morning glories, Ipomoea Alba or Mood Flower is very fragrant. For an extra, almost unseen source of fragrance, sow a little seed of hardy night scented stock and mignonette. Their flowers are inconspicuous but the plants are well worth growing for their scent, strong on summer evenings.

Annuals for Decorative Foliage

For those gardeners who love leaf structures, patterns and varied textures, there are a few excellent annuals which can be grown.

Atriplex hortensis or mountain spinach, a hardy annual, is deep wine coloured. It often grows very tall although it can be kept more bushy by judicious pinching out of growing tips. Its dark foliage wonderfully enhances the vivid citrus colours of tagetes, contrasts dramatically with white and pastel tints, harmonizes with reds, rose and pinks. Sow seed where the plants are to remain. Thin out and transplant as needed.

The half hardy *Ricinus communis,* the castor oil plant, grows to shrub size. This species is 1.5m (5ft) tall and has green leaves, but R.c. Gibsoni is shorter and more handsome with its bronze foliage, while another variety, Impala, is a harmony of bronze, wine and carmine. Best sown early indoors, but seeds may be sown individually outdoors in late spring.

A good stand-in for conifers is the neat half-hardy *Kochia Childsii* or burning bush, so called because it turns colour so dramatically at the end of summer. A new variety, Acapulco Silver, is variegated. It, too, turns colour. The seed often does best sown directly where the plants are to grow.

The beautiful, downy, silver-leaved *Cineraria maritima,* sometimes called *Senecio maritima,* and its varieties, are really half hardy perennials but they are treated as half hardy annuals.

There is a very attractive little nasturtium or tropaeolum, with its light green leaves prettily splashed and marbled with creamy white, sometimes so variegated as almost to appear white-leaved. The plants therefore are decorative from the time they have produced a few leaves. When they flower they are further decorated with pretty little nasturtiums in the familiar bright colours.

Biennials for Spring Colour

Containers need not look bare and desolate in winter and early spring. As we have seen in the section on colourful bulbs (see pp 96–100), bulbs and other kinds of plants – such as conifers, hebes, heathers and biennials, including wallflowers, pansies and double daisies – can be both safely and attractively combined in your containers during the colder weather.

Biennials, and those plants treated as biennials for bedding purposes, are sown one year, usually in late spring, to flower the following year. After they have flowered they die or, if they

1. Pinks (*Dianthus*), in variety. Annuals and perennials. Height: 15–30cm (6in–1ft). Flowers in spring and summer. Sow seed in spring or take cuttings in summer.

2. Lily (*Lilium*), in variety. Perennial. Height: 30cm–2m (1–6ft), according to kind. Flowers in summer in partial shade. Plant bulbs in spring or autumn.

3. Sword lilies (*Gladioli*), in variety. Perennial. Height 43–90cm (1ft 5in–3ft). Flowers late spring, summer and early autumn in sun. Plant bulbs in late spring.

4. Clarkia (*Clarkia elegans*), in great variety. Hardy annual. Height: 30–40cm (1–1ft 6in). Flowers in summer in sun. Sow seed outdoors in autumn or late spring.

5. Livingstone daisies (*Mesembryanthemum criniflorum*), in variety. Half-hardy annual. Height: 8–15cm (3–6in). Flowers in summer sun. Sow seed outdoors under glass in spring.

6. Pot marigolds (*Calendula officinalis*), in variety. Hardy annual. Height: 30–60cm (1–2ft). Flowers in summer in sun or shade. Sow seed outdoors in autumn or spring.

7. Petunias, hybrids in great variety. Half-hardy annual. Height: 20–30cm (8in–1ft). Flowers in summer in sun. Sow seed outdoors under glass in spring.

8. Zinnia, in variety. Half-hardy annual. Height: 15–90cm (6in–3ft). Flowers in summer sun. Sow seed outdoors in spring.

9. Tobacco plant (*Nicotiana grandiflora*), in variety. Half-hardy annual. Height: 60cm–1.2m (2–4ft) Flowers in summer in sun. Sow seed outdoors under glass in spring.

10. Geranium (*Pelargonium*), in great variety. Tender shrubby perennial grown as an annual. Height: 30–60cm (1–2ft). Flowers in summer to early autumn. Plant seed outdoors under glass in early spring to flower the same year, or take cuttings in late summer or autumn to flower the following year.

11. Dwarf sweet peas (*Lathyrus odoratus*), several varieties. Hardy annual. Height: 30–40cm (1–1ft 4in). Flowers in summer in sun. Sow seed outdoors in mid-spring, or under glass outdoors in late winter/early spring.

12. Nasturtiums (*Tropaeolum majus* and *T.nanum*), and varieties – climbing and dwarf. Height: 2m (6ft) and 15cm (6in) respectively. Hardy annual. Flowers in summer in sun. Sow seed outdoors in spring in poor soil for more flowers.

are really perennials, as a few are, they remain untidy and unproductive for the rest of the year. For this reason they are normally removed from pots, tubs and window boxes as soon as the flowers have faded, in time for summer bedding plants to take over. Ideally, biennials should be planted out in late autumn to become hardened during the winter so that they are well established before flowering and, of course, also fill your containers throughout the darkest days of the year. Incidentally, do ensure that their soil does not become dry during this period; regular watering is just as important in colder weather as it is in summer.

These plants can be bought in garden centres and nurseries if

With the warmer days of summer, the flowers that can be container-grown are more varied, will bloom for longer and have stronger perfume. The most fragrant are the lilies, nicotiana (tobacco plants), sweet peas and pinks.

you have little space to raise them from seed yourself, but they do tend to get snapped up rapidly. So, even though some problems may present themselves, it is certainly worth considering the possibility of raising a few biennials for yourself, or perhaps asking a friend with a larger garden or a greenhouse to do so for you. All of these plants are quite hardy, which means that you do not have to find house room for them. Perhaps you could create a tiny garden centre area somewhere in which the seedlings could grow in individual pots until you are ready to plant them.

If you do this you would be certain of having a few of the kinds less likely to be seen on sale. For instance, there are new, vividly coloured, extra large double daisies or *Bellis perennis* and among the dwarf wallflowers, Brilliant Mixed Bedder is recommended for exposed positions, although all the dwarf varieties should be fairly safe. The mixed varieties include some unusual and lovely hues as well as the familiar red and gold. There are also forget-me-nots or myosotis. There are varieties with more than one hue of blue to choose and also a carmine red and a white. Winter flowering pansies in yellow, blue and red harmonies are extremely hardy, strong enough to bloom in the snow. Brompton stocks, the winter flowering variety, bring summer fragrance. Polyanthus and primroses, both now available in a wonderful range of colours, are really perennials, but these also can be treated as winter and spring bedding plants if you sow the seed in early summer. And think how lovely any of these will look intermingled with daffodils and tulips.

Climbing Annuals

If you have no wall or fence space to spare, consider buying prefabricated supports, or making tripods of canes or even wigwams of twiggy sticks to support a display of climbing plants. Bear in mind that any plant which grows upwards extends the total area of display and so adds to your garden space. If you do not particularly want climbers, many plants will cascade downwards prettily also.

Cobea scandens, the cup and saucer flower, needs to climb. It is more vigorous than most annual climbers. It has large, bell-shaped, green-violet flowers from mid summer to autumn. Sow seed indoors in early spring in individual pots.

Dolichos lablab, known also as the hyacinth bean, is an easily grown half hardy annual. It has scented clusters of purple and white flowers from mid-summer to early autumn, followed by ornamental bean-shaped seedpods which are edible.

Morning glories come into the list of Ipomoea species, of which there are many varieties. As well as being attractive climbing plants — the vivid blue flowers seen against a white wall can be breathtaking — they are suitable for hanging baskets. Sow the seeds in warmth in early spring.

Sweet peas, *Lathyrus odoratus,* grow well on roofs and balconies so long as you can give them fairly deep soil and keep them well watered and fed. There are many dwarf varieties such as Snoopea and Bijou, so be sure to check if you want the climbing varieties.

Maurandia barclaiana is a half hardy perennial treated as a half hardy annual. It is a lovely, fairly rare climber, yet it can be grown from seed. It flowers in summer and has foxglove-like blooms varying from white through rose to purple. Some seedsmen also list *M. erubescens,* which has rosy-purple blooms and is ideal for a sunny wall.

You will get flowers, fruits and seeds from a balsam pear by the name of *Momordica charantia,* all of them unusual. The flowers are yellow, spotted with brown and the fruits are strange and wart-covered. These burst when ripe to reveal brightly coloured seeds. Sow the seeds singly in small pots in early spring and protect from the cold.

Black-eyed Susan, *Thunbergia elata,* is not a vigorous or rampant climber, but is useful for hanging baskets as it cascades downwards in such an attractive manner. Its little flat flowers are unusual. Once only the orange kind was grown, but there are now several others, including a very attractive and fragrant white variety.

The nasturtiums include some pleasant climbers. The common climbing variety is rampant and is best grown on a bank or on a patch of poor soil where the plants will flower abundantly. Better for containers are *Tropaeolum lobbianum,* Spitfire and *T. peregrinum,* the Canary creeper.

The latter will clothe a wall or fence if given some support. Its flowers are smaller and different in shape, though because of their numbers, no less showy than the others. The semi-climbing, sweet scented Gleam varieties are best for hanging baskets. There is one drawback to nasturtiums: they play host to blackfly and can become infested in an ugly manner, so watch for this and spray with a systemic insecticide as soon as any are seen.

Nasturtiums trail, creep and climb to decorate this interesting coal-hod container. They flourish in poor soil; a rich soil will produce leaves rather than flowers.

Shrubs and Small Trees

There is one group of really attractive shrubs — the so-called silver-leaved plants, some of which are downy, even woolly, and others which are tougher in texture, light grey or grey-green. Most are evergreen, or should we say evergray. Many have pungent or aromatic leaves; sage, lavender rosemary and artemisia are examples. If your small scale garden is by the sea where there are salt breezes and spray, they will stand up to these conditions.

Many of them will sprawl and are thus ideal for softening the rim of a container or the face of a low wall. It is possible to train them to grow downwards by tieing a small weight to their shoots.

All of the following silver-leaved plants prefer a well drained soil, and so large, properly filled containers will be suitable. Try to give them the shelter of a warm wall, preferably away from direct early morning sunlight, for after frosts they are best kept out of the sun for some hours.

Artemisia abrotanum, or Southernwood, grows to 60-120cm (2-4ft) tall, has pretty, feathery foliage and is delightfully scented.

Convolvulus cneorum is not a climber, as its name suggests, but a neat little bush some 60cm (2ft) tall with pale pink flowers.

Lavendula vera, the Dutch lavender, and *L. lanata* are the most silvery leaved forms, but all lavenders relish the warm sunshine and will grow well in containers or among paving stones. Some will trail prettily if planted near an edge. You have the bonus of masses of sweetly scented flowers. *L. nana atropurpurea*, also known as Hidcote, is dwarf with deep purple flowers.

Santolina chamaecyparissus, cotton lavender. All the species are silver except *S. virens*. A neat, compact variety is *S.c. nana*. *S. neapolitana*, sometimes called *S. rosmarinifolia*, is whiter, its growth looser, with attractive feathery foliage, growing to about 60cm (2ft). Cut back in mid-spring to ensure new shoots.

Among the senecio species is *S. maritima*, usually treated as an annual and lovely for window boxes and hanging baskets. It will only overwinter in a really sheltered site. The more bushy and woodier senecio have different shaped, oval leaves, beautifully soft and downy on the undersides. The long, dainty sprays of flower buds are also downy.

Senecio laxifolius forms a neat, round bush and Dunedin Hybrid Sunshine is an attractive modern variety, growing to a little more than 1m (3ft). This genus has many lovely and varied silver plants, so keep a look out for any of them. All grow well in tubs and other containers.

Teucrium fruticans is a good tenant for a roof or balcony. It will grow to 60cm (2ft) and more. The stems and undersides of the leaves are covered with a silvery-white down. The summer clusters of flowers are a speedwell blue. It needs some protection in winter.

The following, most of which are evergreen in habit though not necessarily in colour, are tough plants which can be grown to protect other more sensitive plants from the wind.

Aucuba japonica, the spotted laurel and its handsome varieties. You need male and female plants if you would like them to bear the vivid red berries. The large, glossy leaves are beautifully variegated with yellow, either speckled with it as in *A. j. variegata* or yellow-centred as in *picturata.*

Euonymus japonicus is one of the many evergreen spindle trees, said to be tolerant of salt spray and smog. *E. j. aureopictus* has vividly variegated foliage. Some plants climb or trail and one which does both is *E. j. colorata,* whose glossy green leaves assume purple tones once the weather turns cool. *E. fortunei* has several very attractive varieties from which you can choose.

Colutea arborescens, or bladder senna, is a member of the pea family with lovely foliage. Its bright yellow flowers form silky swollen pods. This plant will flourish under arid conditions. It will grow to some 3m (10ft), but can be kept within more reasonable bounds by annual hard pruning in spring.

Olearia haastii, the familiar daisy bush, is really half silver, its leaves being green above and silver beneath. The fragrant daisies are produced in masses from early summer onwards. *O. macrodonta,* the New Zealand holly, with large, leathery, sage green leaves, will confront any gale and bloom profusely.

Spartium junceum is the Spanish broom and has fragrant flowers.

Viburnum tinus is an excellent evergreen plant for growing in both shade and cold winds. It flowers during the winter months.

Further evergreens in this list are buxus or box; *Choisya ternata,* the Mexican orange blossom with glossy trefoil foliage and sweetly scented flowers; the gorgeous rock roses or cistus, just the plants for hot, dry places and exposed seaside sites; the interesting little *Corokia cotoneaster,* or wire netting bush; *Coronilla glauca,* an attractive member of the pea family with scented yellow flowers; eucalyptus; *Garrya elliptica,* evergreen, bearing long, beautifully shaped catkins in winter and early spring, a good plant for the colder aspects; *Griselina littoralis,* so tolerant of salty winds;

ilex or holly; ligustrum or privet, of which there are some beautiful variegated forms, including Tricolour, which has white bordered leaves tinged with pale magenta pink when young; *Mahonia aquifolium*; pittosporum; *rosemarinus* or rosemary, these three all evergreens; *Skimmia japonica*, with aromatic foliage and bright red berries — if you make sure you plant both male and female; the invaluable evergreen hebes or shrubby veronica, of which a selection can give you blossom over several months from spring to autumn; and the handsome, sculptural yuccas.

There are so many good conifers which grow well in containers that the gardener might well be recommended simply to grow what appeals, but not all can take strong winds. Those known to do well include the lovely *Chamaecyparis lawsoniana* and *Cupressus macrocarpa*, although they may eventually outgrow their containers and need replacing with smaller specimens.

Perennial Climbers

Although ground space may be limited, small scale gardeners often have some wall space. Even if this is only one wall of a building rising from a paved area it can still provide a home for plants and, when well covered, will add to the entire area of the garden.

A surprising number of climbers will grow in containers placed close to a wall. Using a large container for a thin, upward growing plant will not look attractive unless it is also planted with scramblers and trailers at its edges.

Aristolochia macrophylla is known as the Dutchman's pipe because of the shape of the flowers. It is a vigorous climber which can be kept well under control when grown in a container. Use it for any but really hot sunny walls. Its unusual shaped flowers are brown and yellow-green, appearing in early summer. This climber is also distinguished by its handsome, large, heart-shaped leaves.

Clematis do surprisingly well on roofs and balconies so long as their roots are shaded by other plants, not a difficult thing to

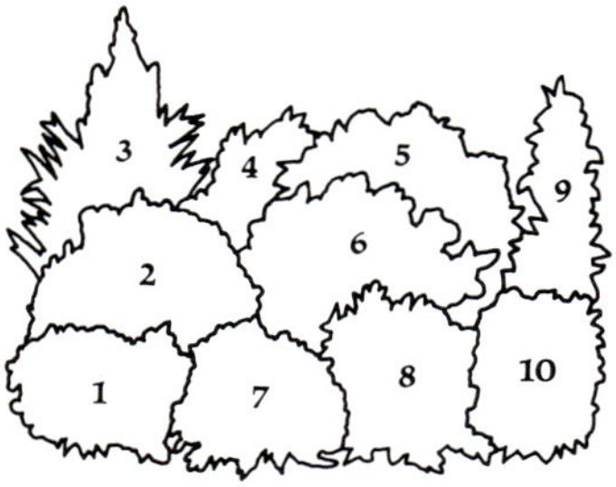

1. Camellia (*Camellia japonica*), in variety. Evergreen shrub. Height: no more than 1.2m (4ft) if container-grown. Flowers in spring; prefers shade and an acid soil.

2. Rose of Sharon or St John's Wort (*Hypericum*). Evergreen and deciduous shrubs. Height: 15–45cm (6in–1 ft 6in). Flowers late summer and early autumn, according to species, in sun and partial shade.

3. Yucca (*Yucca filamentosa*), in variety. Evergreen shrub. Height: 1–2m (3–6ft). Flowers in summer in sun. Can be grown from cuttings taken in mid-spring after frosts.

4. Senecio (*Senecio greyi*). Evergreen shrub with silvery foliage. Height: 1–1.2m (3–4ft). Flowers in summer in sun.

5. Rhododendron, in great variety. Evergreen and deciduous shrubs. Height: 1m (3ft) upwards, many growing into small trees. Flowers in early spring and summer in sun or partial shade. Requires acid soil.

6. Hydrangea (*Hydrangea macrophylla*), and varieties. Deciduous shrub. Height: 1–1.5m (1–4ft 11in). Flowers in summer in sun or partial shade. Blooms are pink or red in limy soil, blue in acid soil.

7. Hebe, in great variety. Evergreen shrub. Height: 30cm–2m (1ft–6ft). Flowers in summer in sun; needs sheltered position.

8. Flowering quince (*Chaenomeles japonica*), and others, including cultivars. Evergreen and deciduous shrubs. Height: 1–2m (3–6ft). Flowers in spring in sun or partial shade.

9. Clematis, in great variety. Deciduous and evergreen climber. Height: 2–3m (6–9ft). Flowers in spring and summer in sun or partial shade, but roots must be in shade. Plant in limy soil.

10. Miniature rose, in variety. Height: 30cm–1m (1–3ft). Flowers in summer in sun. Plant bare-root roses in winter and spring, but not in frozen soil.

ensure in small gardens where plants are placed close together. *C. jackmanii* is a popular deciduous species with deep purple flowers, although the name also covers hybrids such as Nelly Moser, which has pinkish-white flowers with a carmine bar on each petal. *C. armandii* is evergreen and has pretty white flowers.

Clianthus puniceus is also known as Red Cardinal, the parrot's bill or lobster claw, because of the shape of the glossy red flowers which are produced in summer in attractive nodding clusters. It is an evergreen and will grow only in a warm place.

Eccremocarpus scaber has long clusters of orange-red tubular flowers from late spring onwards, fern-like leaves and delicate tendrils. It is easily raised from seed and may also be bought from most garden centres. Semi-woody, it grows quickly on a sheltered wall, even in shallow soil so long as this is rich. It is a true perennial, but is not always hardy and so is more often treated as an annual.

The strong growth of perennial shrubs and some climbers brings a sense of permanence to plant containers and also adds colour and interest. It's inexpensive to buy them and easier than raising them yourself. Plant at any time, except when the soil is frozen.

Hedera or ivy is self-clinging. The familiar wild plant gives no hint of the great variety which can be found in cultivation. It grows in any aspect and is especially valuable for shady areas. Although it readily climbs, you can also use the plants to drape and to carpet. The very large green leaved varieties such as *H. hibernica* bring a touch of the jungle to a garden scene, but if you want colour, choose one with yellow and green variegation. These range from tiny-leaved Little Diamond to *H. canariensis variegata*, also known as Gloire de Marengo.

Hydrangea petiolaris, like ivy, is a clinging climber with large, flat, lacy clusters of flowers which bloom in early summer. It grows well on a shady wall and dislikes sunny places.

Jasminum nudiflorum, winter jasmine, is unscented, but its value lies in the fact that it blooms from late autumn to early spring. If you have no vertical space, use it as a drape, for it is beautifully effective when growing downwards. For perfume grow the white, summer-flowering *J. officinale* or the less vigorous but equally sweetly scented *J.o. stephanense*, with pale pink flowers.

So long as you keep its roots in the shade and see that it never goes dry, the lonicera or honeysuckle will reward you with sweetly scented flowers followed by red berries. The Early Dutch will provide colour and scent in late spring and early summer. Late Dutch flowers in late summer or early autumn and there are others if you would like to make a collection.

Parthenocissus, sometimes called ampelopsis, is the group of plants familiarly known as Virginia creepers. If you have no objection to fallen leaves in autumn, these are plants which can quickly bring a special atmosphere to an enclosed space, for they rapidly cover walls and fences. The lovely clinging species whose bright green glossy leaves grow from coral coloured stems and turn the most vivid hues in the autumn is *P. tricuspidata*, often listed as *A. veitchii*. It will grow well in any aspect. For really theatrical drapery, grow *P. quinquefolia*. You may find this listed as *A. quinquefolia* or *Vitis hederacea* (nomenclature can be very confusing). This will climb as well as trail. Another, *P. henryana*, is daintier and more tender. It should not be planted where it is exposed to cold winds or to early sunlight.

Polygonum baldschuanicum, the Russian or Mile-a-Minute vine, is a very vigorous grower and can easily get out of hand in a ground level garden. Fortunately, when its roots are restricted in a container it behaves more moderately. It is a pleasant plant for an overhead trellis and it looks particularly well intertwined with a parthenocissus. It flowers from summer to autumn — a time when the creamy white blossoms contrast with the vivid leaves of the other plant.

Pyracantha rogersiana and its varieties will grow flat against a wall, as well as freely in bush form in the open. A profusion of yellow, orange or red berries distinguishes this attractive plant.

Solanum jasminoides, the potato vine, is a lovely climber and twiner. Give it a trellis or some kind of strong support and it will grow up easily and beautifully. Its purple, orange stamened flowers are similar to those of the potato.

There are many vines suitable for patio, roof and balcony gardens. The decorative species may suit you better than those grown for their fruit, since these do not need the precise pruning that is necessary for a good crop of grapes. Of the more ornamental types *Vitis coignetiae* will grow in any aspect. A vine which combines both fruit and decoration is *V. vinifera Brandt.* This prefers a sunny situation.

Like all other vigorous plants grown in containers, wisteria is somewhat inhibited when restricted, but nevertheless it will twine and bloom. The best of the species is *W. sinensis*.

Roses are much more adaptable than many gardeners realize. They grow well in large flower pots and in other containers, but need good soil and frequent feeding. The roots should be kept moist. There is a great variety of climbing roses; to mention a few: Danse du Feu has vivid red flowers, Golden Showers, brilliant yellow — as might be expected — and New Dawn's are pink.

Miniature Plants

Conditions on a roof, balcony or patio can sometimes be very similar to those of a rock garden. Alpines are the answer, particularly if space is limited. With their pretty, low shapes and many-coloured flowers, these perennials will grow in shallow, well-drained soil. You can easily provide this in a sink garden or shallow plant container. In confined areas the charm of these delightful little plants is enhanced. Among them are the many varieties of saxifrage, the dianthus pinks, thymus, campanula, sedums and sempervivums. But also consider growing some of the tiny bulbous plants – Doll's House daffoldils, for instance – as well as miniature conifers, roses and fuchsias, dwarf azaleas and rhododendrons, though these latter will only thrive in an acid soil.

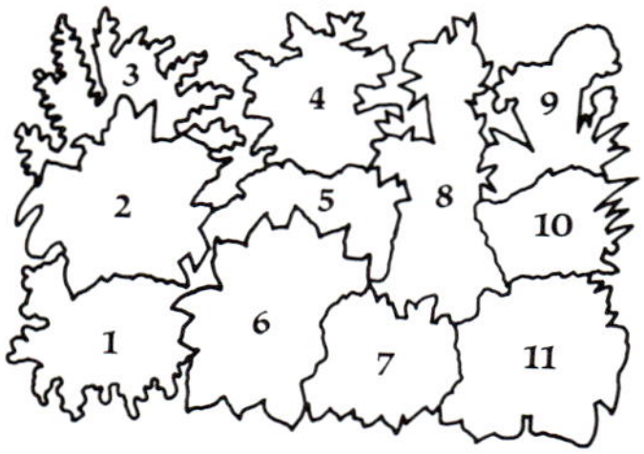

1. Maidenhair fern (*Adiantum*), in variety. Height: 1m (3ft). Tender varieties thrive outside in moist, shady conditions in summer, hardy species all year round in the same conditions.

2. Hart's tongue fern (*Phyllitis scolopendrium*), in variety. Height: 30–60cm (1–2ft). Thrives in moist, shady conditions and will tolerate moderately draughty situations.

3. Hard fern (*Blechnum spicant*), in variety. Height: 15–30cm (6in–1ft). Requires moist shady conditions, will tolerate draughts.

4. Royal fern (*Osmunda regalis*), in variety. Height: 60cm–2m (2–6ft). Grow in moist, shady site. Leaves turn brownish red in autumn.

5. Lady's mantle (*Alchemilla mollis*). Perennial. Height: 30cm (1ft). Tiny yellow flowers in summer, but grown for foliage; will tolerate shade and partial shade. Sow seed outdoors or divide in spring.

6. Plantain lily (*Hosta*), in variety. Height: 30–60cm (1–2ft). Flowers in summer but grown for foliage in partial shade. Divide in autumn or spring when grown too large; or grow from cuttings in spring.

7. Pansy (*Viola*), in great variety. Perennial. Height: 15cm (6in). Flowers in spring, summer and winter, according to type and should be shaded from hot sun. Sow seeds in spring, preferably indoors.

8. Barrenwort (*Epimedium*), in variety. Hardy perennial. Height: 15–35cm (6in–1ft 2in). Flowers in spring, but grown for foliage in shade.

9. African lily (*Agapanthus*), in variety. Perennial. Height: 45–90cm (1ft 6in–3ft). Thrives in sun or shade, the blue flowers giving spring and summer colour to shady sites. Divide in spring or autumn.

10. Campanula, in great variety; trailing and upright species. Height: 8cm (3in) and 43cm (1ft 5in), respectively. Perennials, biennials and annuals. Flowers in summer in partial shade. Sow seed outside in spring or grow from cuttings.

11. Bergenia, in variety. Perennial. Height: 30cm (1ft). Flowers in spring in sun or shade. Grown for its attractive evergreen foliage. Sow seeds outdoors, divide or take cuttings in spring.

Ferns and Plants for Shady Places

There are many species of ferns and some popular and attractive varieties are illustrated. All of them are flowerless and some are hardy enough to grow under arctic conditions, while others are more delicate. Ferns are perennials and most will retain their foliage all year round if grown in temperate climates. Nearly all those commonly grown require cool, moist, shaded conditions. Since smaller containers dry out quickly, it is advisable to grow ferns in larger pots, tubs or troughs, giving

Ferns and certain softer shrubs can thrive in lightly shaded areas where roots can be kept constantly cool and moist. In these conditions, even the tender types of maidenhair fern can enjoy a few weeks outside.

them a moisture-retentive, peaty soil mixture and, if possible, siting them where a down-pipe can trickle a little water on them frequently. Ferns do not like to paddle or be drowned, but it is essential that their roots be kept moist and their foliage away from prolonged exposure to the sun.

Remove any dead leaves or fronds in spring and either divide the plant or repot it when it outgrows its container. Division is also a way of propagating ferns, which is simpler than the lengthy process of growing from spores, so the small scale gardener would be advised to buy his ferns initially and then propagate by division.

A selection of other plants which grow well with ferns in shady places is also illustrated. Some are grown for their flowers, such as pansies, African lilies and campanulas, which will bring much-needed colour to a partially shady site. Other plants are grown for their attractive foliage and these include bergenia and barrenwort. It must be remembered that conifers can also be grown, as can privet and box. Ivies and flowering climbers, such as clematis and honeysuckle, are both decorative and useful in covering walls and pipes in a basement area.

Plants for Protected Places

A fine assortment of plants which cannot be relied on to withstand the weather can be safely grown in the shelter of the plants mentioned on pp 112–13. They are, however, suitable for seaside gardening. They include the varieties of buddleia; *Carpinus betulus*, hornbeam; the pretty blue flowered *Caryopteris clandonensis* or C. Kew Blue, with darker blossom; escallonia, of which there are now many lovely varieties; hardy fuchsias (see below); *Hydrangea macrophylla*, the mop-headed *hortensis* and the daintier lacecaps. These will produce rose, red and pink flowers in limy soils, but in acid soils the blooms are beautifully blue, so you can vary them if you wish. *Potentilla fructicosa*, a member of the rose family, a little shrub which is covered with flowers for a long period and *P. farreri*, have many pretty varieties.

Fuchsias are among the most beautiful of summer flowering shrubs. Only a few of them, sold by nurserymen, are hardy or almost so, and although these can be pretty they are not nearly so spectacular as some of the more tender kinds which have to be over-wintered away from frosts. At the beginning of the bedding season they are on sale everywhere as small plants. Larger specimens may be bought from specialist fuchsia growers, who produce a great number of varieties, some trailing types, ideal for hanging baskets and window boxes, some trained as columns.

Fuchsias are easily raised from cuttings on a window sill and from seeds, which should be sown in spring. Some seed mixtures produce both single and double flowered varieties.

These plants grow best where they can be in shade for a few

hours each day, preferably during the sunniest period. It is important that the roots are not allowed to dry out, or both the flowers and the foliage will drop.

Plants should be kept groomed and dead headed, and should you find seed pods swollen into dark red berries, eat them. Fuchsia fruits, like those of some cacti, are thought by some to be the most delicious in the world.

There are many other lovely shrubs and small trees which are not quite hardy enough to stand fully exposed on all sides to hot sun, strong winds, cold air or frosts. In many cases, these can be grown quite successfully if they are planted close to a wall which affords them protection. Should the winter be very severe they are likely to suffer, but being close to a wall it is usually possible to protect them in some way, with transparent plastic sheeting for instance, until the very cold spell has passed.

Abelia schumannii and *A. grandiflora*, evergreen, will grow to about 1-1.2m (3-4ft) against a sunny wall. They flower from late summer to autumn.

Abeliophyllum distichum, about 2.5m (8ft), not unlike forsythia except that flowers are pink and fragrant.

Abutilon, 2-3m (6-10ft), can be raised from seed. *A. megapotanicum* is evergreen, with orange-red flowers from spring onwards. *A vitifolium* has downy, vine-shaped leaves and hollyhock-like mauve flowers.

Acacea dealbata, mimosa, grows to 3m (10ft) or more but can be kept under control in a container. Once it flowers it should be cut back. If frosted, it will shoot again from the base.

Evergreen ceanothus are of greater value to the small scale gardener than the deciduous species and do well against a sunny wall. There are many to choose from and all flower in early summer except *C. burkwoodii* and Autumnal Blue.

The lovely flowering quince, chaenomeles, also does well in full sun against a wall. It flowers early and has large, orange-scarlet blossoms; the fruits can be used for making jelly.

Fremontodendron californicum, 3m (10ft), a beautiful plant, with the shoots and undersides of the leaves covered in a russet fur. Give it a sunny wall and it will flower continually throughout the summer.

Lippia citriodora, 2.5m (8ft), the true scented verbena, with evergreen, lemon-scented leaves and lavender flowers in summer.

Plumbago capensis, 3-5m (10-15ft), with soft blue flowers, can be kept small and compact when container grown.

Although camellias make particularly suitable free-standing tub plants, they grow well with the protection of a wall; they should not be in a position where they are exposed to the morning sun after frosts, as this may destroy the blooms. They will not tolerate winds or a limy soil. Their flowers are double or single in red, pink, white or variegated. Adolphe Audusson (red), Gloire de Nantes (pink), Nobilissima (double white) and Apollo (red flecked with white) are popular varieties.

Several fruits grow well on patios, such as dwarf standard apples, black currants, gooseberries and strawberries. Though the fruit may not be plentiful, they do look attractive.

Most popular herbs are easy and quick to grow in window boxes or pots, from the tall angelica to the small thymes and spiky chives. All are aromatic and worth growing, whether for use in the kitchen or not.

Vegetables, Fruit and Herbs

Few foods taste as good as those you have grown yourself, but an added bonus is that some vegetables also make handsome climbing annuals. Perhaps the most versatile are the climbing beans, both the runner and the French varieties. Painted Lady, a runner bean, has red and white flowers and Sunset's flowers are pink. Any of the more usual scarlet flowered varieties are extremely attractive when seen against white walls, the handsome green foliage and the scarlet flowers complementing each other perfectly. The purple-podded climbing bean has burnished, violet-green foliage which harmonizes attractively with the lilac flowers and the deep purple pods, which turn a delicious looking jade green when cooked. Selma Zebra is also coloured with purple, but its pods are attractively speckled.

Good patio plants are those of the cucurbita tribe: all the gourds, such as cucumbers, squash and pumpkins. All are splendid plants and most are vigorous climbers. Their great yellow trumpet flowers are very showy. They are half hardy and can be raised indoors, or the seed can be sown outside *in situ* in early summer.

Yellow and red tomatoes, green, yellow and red peppers, purple or white striped aubergines, add both colour and interest to the scene. There are varieties specially bred for container gardeners; for instance, tomatoes such as Minibel, only 30cm (1ft) tall, bearing an early crop of small fruits, just the plants for window boxes, and Twiggy, a yellow sweet pepper, ideal for pots. Generally speaking, any vegetable that will grow in a cold greenhouse in summer can also be grown in a container outdoors in a warm and sheltered place.

When any of these are grown in large containers or in growbags, see if you can make space close to the edges of the holder for a crop from some other, smaller plant. There lettuce seedlings can be pricked out, radishes, beetroot, parsley, chervil or basil sown thinly. When these are harvested they should not disturb the roots of the longer-lived plants in the centre.

Almost all tree fruits can be pot grown, although they will never produce a great crop, but they do give blossom as well as fruit and so are rewarding in this respect. In winter and early spring their buds and blossoms should be protected against birds with nets.

A strawberry barrel is an interesting feature in a small space garden (see pp 68–70). Specialists sell certain varieties best suited to this style of fruit cultivation and the tiny alpine strawberries can also be grown this way. These also are attractive little plants to grow in pots, tubs or window boxes.

All the shrubby herbs are good container plants; indeed, the bay is more often seen in a tub than growing in open land. Rosemary, sage, thyme and winter savory are nicely evergreen and can be fitted in to any scheme. Mints and tarragon will grow in pots, but they are not so attractive, but even so it can be worthwhile to find a place in the shade for them. Fennel will grow in a large flower pot or some other container, as will dill. Be sure that the soil does not dry out for any of these.

If you use plenty of herbs in cooking you will soon denude any plants you have. The evergreen, shrubby kinds should therefore be allowed to grow to a good size before they are cut. If you have space, keep a few pots continuously sown with the quick maturing kinds such as basil, chervil, coriander, parsley and sweet marjoram. Sow a pinch of seed at intervals so that as one pot is cut another is ready. Chives can also be treated this way.

INDEX

♦

Figures in brackets refer to illustrations